ALL IN A NUTSHELL

ALL IN A NUTSHELL

Creation

Transmutation of Consciousness

Evolution of The Cosmic Cell

A Way of Life

BY

ARMELLA MARIE WHITNEY

ISBN# 1-58721-250-1

A profound thank you to President Timothy Jacobs,
who founded 1st Books Library; opening the door to
new authors and other by giving them an
opportunity to use their budding talents, and to Rich
Van Lue, Associate Director of Author Services of
1st Books Library.

1stBooks-rev.11/15/00

A special tribute is given to:

The late Dr. Walter Russell, whose books, "The Secret of Light"and "A New Concept of The Universe," changed my life and understanding of the Universe and my place in it.

He and his wife, Lao, joined minds to write a Course on Natural Law, Science, and Philosophy, in which they explain the new concepts in easy to understand language.

Their teachings, spread throughout the world through many study groups, have heightened the concept of Love as the basis of all creation and relationships.

The University was co-founded by the late Dr. Walter and Lao Russell. It was formerly the Walter Russell Foundation.

Dr. Russell is also known as "The Man Who Tapped The Secret of The Universe."

Present address is:

University of Science and Philosophy
P.O. Box 520
Waynesboro, VA 22980

"Will You Join Us?"

* * * *

A bouquet of Blessings to Laara Lindo, who is now President and CEO of the University of Science and Philosophy, who has honored this book with a place in the University Book Store.

About the Book

Dear Reader:

At this period in time, as our consciousness unfolds, we are rediscovering our True Self. This story is about how the unfoldment takes place in your daily life.

Come along with us in this adventure of ALL IN A NUTSHELL, as we explore how the process of transmutation of the cosmic cell and Consciousness has been going on since the beginning of time until it has reached its' present form in the human body.

It is as important to know this as is going to grade school before entering college. For, as our Consciousness or awareness of life unfolds, we are better able to understand life and to think for ourselves. This releases us from the instinctual control of Nature to become Master of our own life.

In these unique and interesting chapters of ALL IN A NUTSHELL, we have woven together the many facets of life from the many viewpoints of Science, Spiritual beliefs, Philosophy and others, to show how they all work together to make up the interesting story of your daily life, because this is where it all takes place.

We discuss how our thoughts, feelings and emotions are recorded in the bookkeeping system of God's (the Creator) Mind, just as our memories are impressed on our mind; just as a camera records your picture on its film. This keeps us in constant contact with the Creator.

In some other chapters we explain how our mind and body are "constructed and connected" to the invisible dimension of Soul and Spirit to bring forth our wishes and dreams; our invisible cube of light home that surrounds us; and how rhythm and the law of balance work together bringing harmony into our life.

Our first three chapters set the stage for the scientific explanation of the colorful chapters that follow.

As these new levels of awareness unfold to us, our extra sensory perception expands, and our intuition and ability to create a better life increases; always keeping in mind that as each new level of awareness unfolds itself to us, it also reveals itself to be the Truth.

Acknowledgements

To Treasured Friends:

Jana Cloward and Prof. Helen Yanko, whose suggestions were gratefully accepted, and to all those whose life long friendships fashioned ideas that contributed to these chapters.

* * * *

To my dear family whose patience was tried as I practiced this daily Wisdom.

* * * *

To my Grandson Jeff, whose patient typing brought to fruition these chapters.

* * * *

And last - - -

To the Knower within who generously impressed me with fresh sounding phrases to express age old truths.

* * * *

A warm thank you to:

Prof. Nancy Ramsey for her excellent proof reading.
To Anna Maria and my Grandchildren Paula and David for the use of their computers.

* * * *

Finally, to my daughter, Cindi, for the format and the final typing for publishing.

Dedication

Dedicated to my beloved Teachers, the late:

Bula G. Williams

Dr. Walter Russell

J. Campbell Bonner

Dr. Fritz Kunkel

Sara Robbins

Some of those among the many in the 1940's whose fingers of Light broke ground for the sprouting of the New Age of Man.

* * * *

CONTENTS

CHAPTER

1	Creation
2	Thoughts and The Invisible Gasses
3	Cells – Our Garment of Protection
4	The Elephant
5	A Nod To The Dinosaurs
6	And Now Man
7	Today's World
8	The Eyes of God
9	Rhythm Is Our Business
10	The One Mind
11	Our Body and Its Components
12	Earth – Variations of A Theme
13	Soul and Spirit
14	The Heavens Declare The Glory of The Lord
	Some Afterthoughts
	Poem - I Plucked A String
	Bibliography

Introduction

Though it seems everything has been said before – how it is given to each Individual, as their consciousness unfolds – is new.

This is written in an attempt to convey, in a simple condensed and understandable manner, the inter-relatedness of all of Creation with each other, from the beginning, to this present day, reestablishing contact with our past, and a wondering peek at our yet unknown future.

To do this, may I share with you a few of the main ideas of the why, how it works, and some suggestions of what to do about it, as the Transformation takes place within us, as well as the world about us.

To those who may not have had time to browse – but have wondered what it's all about – may it conjure a picture and awareness of the overall purpose of life, and that life has a Goal, and that goal is to bring about harmony and love to all Mankind.

* * * *

The Adventure of Transmutation

Who are you?

You are <u>not</u> your body.

YOU ARE THE CENTER OF A GROUP OF COSMIC CELLS!

You are the Spirit-the Light that created and runs the body.

The Universe is composed of electric waves of light created by the thinking of the Creator-God.

We create our bodies with light as God creates his body-which is the Universe.

When we think, we create electrical wave vibrations that attract the necessary particles of energy to collect into a solid mass to objectify our creations-our body-or any other objects, to manifest our ideas.

Your creations are <u>exactly</u> what you are aware of as an individual unit of consciousness. Consciousness is your degree of <u>awareness</u> of God in you.

Electric waves of light are created by the motion of your thinking.

Electric waves are composed of positive and negative states of motion.

The balancing of the positive and negative states of motion is determined by the level of balance we have attained through growth of consciousness.

We can choose the level from which we want to live.

There are levels visible and invisible, each influences the other.

The invisible levels are our thoughts and ideas.

The idea promotes thought-thought creates motion and motion solidifies matter into objects or the manifestation of your world as you know it.

We each create our own consequences and rewards.

Your body's illnesses or health are the results of all <u>you</u> have created from past lifetimes as well as this lifetime.

What you do in this life determines the beauty or problems that will manifest in your next life's pattern. Some of what you are manifesting in this life are the results of past mistakes and/or successes.

You can determine your success as well as your downfall-through working moment to moment with the Spirit within you-or alone.

Working with the spirit within brings about Balance to all unbalanced situations in your life.

Unbalance is any situation that is <u>less</u> than Peace and Happiness in your life.

Through the balancing of the opposites of positive and negative we raise the Consciousness of the cells of our body. The Consciousness is the part of God within us.

The purpose of raising the Consciousness is to come into a state of Peace and Joy, which is the Sole Purpose of Creation.

All things begin at their base and work upward to their crown.

The base of the body is the sex organs-the crown is the top of the head.

In our transmutation of the cell, we transmute the energy of the lower sex center to the highest Mental and Spiritual centers in the head.

This is called by many names-but the Journey always has the same beginning and ending-from the base of the body to the crown of the head. It is an essential requirement to graduate from this Earth Planet.

By transmutation is <u>meant</u> purifying all unhealthy egotistical self-indulgence for pleasure, misuse of good for evil, using life for one's selfish purpose.

Transmutation <u>is</u> raising up every negative thought, word, action, and desire to its highest level of expression.

It may take a day, a week, or many lifetimes, as <u>you</u> please

* * * *

Having received this intuitive Message, the Story seemed to formulate itself – weaving the ideas and wisdom gained from learning, practicing, and revelations experienced during fifty years of study.

Recorded:

December 24, 1991
12:40 p.m.

And this is the story. . . . .

1
Creation

In the Beginning, in the Stillness, there was only God.

The Still invisible Magnetic Light of All Knowing Mind was He.

In the Light of Mind was the Divine Seed Idea for all Creation.

Centered in the invisible Stillness was the Holy Word-The Supreme Power of the Creator.

"Of what use is an idea without someone to share it?"

So God thought, and a myriad of images flowed through His Mind as He joyously dreamed His Creation into a form.

The Plan and Purpose of the entire drama gathered momentum within His Mind: stars, suns, earths, animals, and creatures of every size and shape, until finally all the images were perfect and in order.

"And who will enjoy all this beauty, He mused?"

"Someone like unto Myself, who will lovingly care for and carry on my creation."

"I will prepare a place for him, this Grand Man, who will be made in my own Image and Likeness."

Now, God is a volatile Creator, full of Life, Love, Intelligence, Wisdom, Power, and humor as well.

So inbreathing deeply, He gathered together His forces and with a vast and Mighty pressure, a breath of explosive gaseous energy burst forth from that Still Center and thrust the entire Universe of matter and motion into being.

The first outward Breath of Creation was born.

"LET THERE BE LIGHT!" He thundered, AND THERE WAS LIGHT!

The powerful thought waves of rainbow colored lights sprang forth from His Mind, spun into space and whirled with wild abandonment.

As He spoke, A Mighty Power moved throughout the darkness and separated the earth from the heavens.

MOTION SEPARATED ITSELF FROM STILLNES AND BECAME FORM.

The tumultuous reeling of gases as they gave impetus to the waves of flashing many colored lights and thunderous waves of Sound, each with it's own tone, echoed throughout all of space, a Divine Symphony, as matter wound itself into spirals of energy that adjusted to the <u>specific pressures</u> determined for them by the Light, to form the worlds upon which all Creation would be birthed. ----

The intensity of light created by your thinking determines the shape and size of all your creations, as did God's.

The "I" surrounded Itself with matter and became Visible.

The Word became Flesh and dwelt amongst us.

Male and Female created He them, equal and opposite in His own Image and Likeness created He them.

The woman bearing the Light within, and the man caring for her.

Into the darkness went the Light, knowing Itself as Perfect Being, God, the darkness yielding to the Light,

The shadows created by the Light as they touched the darkness of space, danced merrily in the ethers, and the Lord saw that it was good.

The Lord being the one made flesh.

Some shadows became distorted and some were perfect, but all shadows were but <u>images</u> in the Mind of the Creator.

What wonders were in the Heavens as He brought forth His Majestic Masterpiece!

Oh, the Glories of Creating this One Grand Cosmic Play---

The Universal Dance of the Atoms.

In this manner came the Universe into being that God might know Himself in Action.

* * * *

How long this Grand and mysterious event in time went on one cannot imagine-but this first outward breath gave Life to all there was to be---

This was the beginning of the Universal Pump, the breath of God, which was to breathe out and in, in every star, atom and body that would henceforth be formed and birthed into the visible world.

ALL FASHIONED FROM THE INVISIBLE GASEOUS BREATH OF GOD

The breath we breathe in and out each moment is our lifeline to God. We are breathed out at birth with an allotted amount of energy, to be used 'till our work on earth is finished. Then God withdraws his breath, the inward breath, and we return to the invisible world of Light-Heaven-where we function in our Light body, as Jesus did upon appearing to His disciples in His Glorified Light body after the Resurrection, then our physical body returns to the gases and elements from which it came, to be recycled for creation of other bodies.

"Dust thou art and to dust thou shalt return," refers to our physical cell body. The Spirit lives forever.

THE LAW OF CONSERVATION-NOTHING IS EVER LOST ONLY RECONSTRUCTED

Throughout this vast period of the churning and seething of the elements as they were being wrought into forms, shaped by the Idea in the Creator's Mind, and under the Balancing Pressures of positive and negative lights of motion, which were to be His Laws of Balance for the protection of all life and beings who were to inhabit the earth as a School of Learning; there came into being, Suns, the primary Centers, carrying the Patterned Seeds of all its' creations, the Fathers of the Universe, the Suns being a physical manifestation of the invisible Light of the Creator.

As rings of gases were whirled from the Sun's equator as it spun in space, they were molded into spheres by the polarizing motion of positive and negative electric thought waves, weaving their threads of light into patterns.

For eons this shaping of spheres went on, like unto a Potter molding his clay bowl.

Till one day-in the far distant past, after the Great Intelligence had spoken Creation into existence, in that special moment, when molding had formed the earth's mountains and lowlands in which water could rest from it's rushing turmoil, and be warmed by the rays of the sun, the <u>patterned seed forms</u>, invisible, swirled from the energy of the Sun and implanted themselves within Mother Earth to be nurtured by water, air, and the Cosmic Light of the Sun. In that moment-the first Intelligent cell was birthed in the deep dark oozy cradle of the ocean's bed.

This cell was centered by a still Magnetic Force that attracted all the elements necessary to evolve one day, to form a body in which man, as a thinking, knowing being, could learn to create, control, and direct the elements, and bring forth our world as we know it today.

In that instant, the story of Transmutation was born, and from that day forth the struggle of the pairs of opposites, good and evil, to control man's body, mind and soul began.

This cell was activated by the instinctual urge of DESIRE to divide and multiply until it produced an orderly group of other cells that would enable it to become something other than a single cell, each with it's own still Magnetic Center, the Center where God rests in each of his Creations, an orderly purposeful, conglomerate of cells. Like a Hologram, if broken, each piece contains the complete picture of the original, so each cell has within it the entire picture of it's Creator's idea, but smaller in size. We are all chips off God's one whole Idea of Creation – a perfect replica. How well are we imitating that pattern? And what is the pattern?

Jesus set it forth in His simple, eloquent- "Sermon on the Mount." Do read it.

The instinctual evolutionary force behind this struggle of creating, guided the formation in sequential steps over millions of years until one day, a variety of forms were created and among them the Pattern for the body of man.

This was the beginning of the evolution of the Cosmic Cell-from its inception in the primordial mud of the ocean's bed, to the unknown future and perfection of spiritual man.

During this period of evolving, the cell lived through many experiences: mineral, vegetable, animal, then finally to be used as a structure for man's body. The limbic brain holds the memories of these transitions as well as does the cells of the embryo in its nine months of forming a body.

We must remember again, man's body is not himself, but a form the Spirit works through to accomplish the Play of Creation.

When the cells had evolved sufficiently to function as a human body, it was then God breathed into them the Spirit of Life and they became aware of themselves as separate, Male and Female, the Garden of Eden.

Before that they had functioned by instinct as the animals did, now they were Aware.

When they became Aware, the responsibility for the care of the body and creation began. Caring for and assisting as-Co-Creators with God, they were given Authority over the earth as well as to multiply. At that period of time there were few humans; now we have multiplied to billions. The multiplying as you can see, hasn't faltered; it's knowing how to keep it in Balance that is lagging.

All that ever happens in creating is bringing ideas and forms to life, and then learning how to use and balance them.

The field is your body-home, family, friends, and country, how well you are balancing them shows in the results that take place in your life.

To the degree they were obedient to the Law set up by the Creator, symbolized by the Tree in the Center of Eden, they retained their freedom-but as in the instance of Cain killing Abel (killing being that instinctive urge of the cells' records of the animal experience) the freedom was lost and he was cast out of Paradise and became a fugitive from justice, to wander the face of the earth.

Our guilt at disobeying what we know is right, causes much unhappiness because we injure the Soul, which is our direct connection with God.

We must overcome the <u>negative</u> part of the instinctive urge or it will destroy us.

We must obey this <u>Law of Balance</u>. In this case, only obedience was required as their consciousness was still as that of a child.

As civilization moved forward to a new age of expanded consciousness and understanding, the brain had developed, again, people lost sight of their goal and needed a reminder.

Other teachers were sent such as Moses, Buddha, and the greatest of all, Jesus, to mention a few, to fill the needs and <u>line up the thinking of the human race for that period of time.</u>

We remember Moses and his Ten Commandments, Jesus' Sermon on the Mount, Buddha and his Laws for Society.

The latest Messenger of Light to my knowledge in this Scientific Age is the late Dr. Walter Russell, a Cosmic Conscious Mystic as well as a Scientist. His new Cosmogony's influence, spread throughout the world, testifies to a two-way Perpetual Motion Universe, life interchanging with death to again reborn life.

There is no death.

Death is that period of unawareness between the moment we leave earth and become aware of the invisible world.

To overcome the <u>idea</u> of death is to be <u>conscious</u> of all sequences as you transfer your Consciousness from the physical plane to the invisible dimensions.

The purpose of Dr, Russell's Message is to build that Bridge of Awareness. This takes away the fear and mystery of Transition, a New Concept of the Universe for the new period we're moving into, from which comes the <u>Law of Balance</u>.

Again, we're making a step forward in time.

Are you ready?

Throughout the evolving states of man, our consciousness has developed, living is more complicated, but we are still basically learning **<u>OBEDIENCE</u>**.

To what?

The Law of Balance, which is the Will of God for good, when broken, causes all our problems as well as the worlds.

We go through life ever being watched by the two balancing Eyes of God, as a mother and father watches over a child learning to walk.

THE COSMIC EYE WATCHES AND BALANCES ALL THINGS

We will talk more about the Eyes of Balance later in our discussion.

As we grow into the future we will become ever more aware of the <u>effect</u> this Law has on our lives and hopefully be more willing to obey it. It's the only hope of the world and mankind---

<u>BALANCE</u>

It was said by the Master, "Even greater things ye shall do." but before we get to share them, we must learn as a juggler, to balance, appreciate and use <u>wisely</u> what we already have.

Lack of appreciation and misuse of our lives, keeps our good from us. <u>Free will</u> has its' disadvantages.

"Grateful is my heart O Lord, for all the wonders you have shared with us in your beautiful creation."

The Tree of Life, the center from which the Spirit functions in us, is the nervous system laced throughout our body, and warns us through intuition of right and wrong.

We call it Conscience. If not heeded and used wisely, it will surely destroy our lives and us. Witness our packed prisons and many other world problems-TODAY'S fugitives from justice.

It is through our mistakes we become aware of these opposites of good and evil, and the opportunity to correct them that we may live in Peace and Happiness. A choice which must be made sooner or later for the world's sake as well as our own.

These were the beginning lessons of how to live in harmony with Creation and enjoy a taste of Paradise on earth.

Balance, being symbolized by a Pair of Scales; our lives are constantly weighed in the balance by two moving poles of motion, the positive and negative, the Balancing Arms of God. These arms are affected by every decision we make, the results depending on the act.

THE ACT IS THE LAW

You get in return exactly what you give out in some form at sometime. That's why it is reasonable to assume Reincarnation as a fact. We can't learn it all in one lifetime.

This lifetime is only a short sequence of events, including the entire story of your life-what has been in the long distant past-and what will be in the future-a Serial Story, the difference being you wear a new body for each part in the play, though the cells still carry the old records.

Your free will allows you to change it. Why not start now creating it, as you would like it to be? You are only one decision from success.

To overcome the negative just keep adding to the positive. Like a scale, it will finally come into balance.

No effort is ever lost, but is stored by Law in your Cosmic Bank Account. No one can use it, tax it, or take it from you but <u>yourself</u>-

So-"Come you lost Atoms, to your center draw
Rays that have wandered into Darkness wide,
Return, and back into your sun sub-side."

(The lovely way in which E.T. Fitzgerald expressed it.)

Persistent effort determines your success, see the problem through.

Many of our problems are rooted in what we <u>want</u> to do and be, and what we <u>have</u> to do.

What we have to do, if done well, prepares us for what we want to do-finally we are released and out of bondage. **<u>PATIENCE.</u>**

We have to be willing to do what Life presents to us before we can be freed.

The entire Universal Power works with you, if you get in tune and follow its' laws. It's the On-Track-Engine that takes us to our true destination - <u>Get</u> <u>On</u> <u>Board</u>!

Flow with Life as a tree flows with the wind-it's taking you to your Highest Destiny.

* * * *

In discussing the steps used to create this Universe we turn to an interesting viewpoint given by Alfred Tennyson, Poet Laureate of England in the 1850's.

On a special evening visit with Lord Tennyson, who was nearly eighty, his friend Dr. Joseph Joachim, a Composer and violinist of note, asked what he thought about how Creation began, its purpose and final goal?

To which Tennyson replied, "God is Spirit and Spirits' only attribute is thought, so I see the first ** step as:

Divine thought
Plan and Purpose
Ether
Light
Atoms-God's building blocks
Molecules
Cells from which all living forms have been evolved.

"As for the ultimate goal of creation, is the evolving of the individual centers of Consciousness, which are potentially capable of living forever in another higher realm that Jesus called – "The Kingdom of Heaven."

One God, one law, one element.

And one far off Divine Event.

To which all Creation moves.

From-In Memorium

**Quoted from "Talks with Great Composers" by Arthur Abel.

15

16

2
Thoughts and the Invisible Gases

As we venture deeper into understanding how creating works, we will talk about thoughts, then the Invisible Gasses, which record your thoughts and your entire history since your first cell beginnings, and continue to do so each moment you exist.

First-what is thinking?

Thinking is a response to the <u>Soul's Seed-of Desire</u> within you to acquire knowledge or to create something.

Thinking is the action that releases a two-way motion of positive and negative electrical energy that explodes from a point of <u>Stillness</u> in the Center of your brain, extends itself to the left and right lobes; then these two workers exchange energy with each other, as a battery does, until the energy is depleted and all is still once more, in a state of rest. This is called the cycle of thought-from a point of stillness, when you first have the thought-to a state of motion, while thinking, then a return to stillness when completed.

All creation follows this <u>Law of Cycles:</u> the four seasons, day and night, life and death, sleep and awake; a tree buds, blooms, bears fruit, then goes to sleep for the winter. In the Spring the Cycle starts over again.

The cycles are inevitable-it's Life. Each one's life cycle is determined by the initial impulse of energy with which they were born.

Again, thoughts are light-waves of motion that flow from your mind into space, attracting the necessary atoms, molecules, and other elements to make your dreams come true. Then, they are pumped into visibility by the Universal Pump-the Breath of God – which is also your breath.

All Creation breathes in and out in rhythm with God's breathing-from the tiniest bug to the largest sun, each at its own rate of speed.

All knowledge to create lies in that Still Center in your brain; to know how this works give us better control of our lives.

OUR THOUGHT WORLD IS THE WOMB OF OUR CREATION

What you harbor repeatedly in your thoughts will be given birth to at some time.

We need to know that thoughts create effects on different levels: physical, emotional, and mental. They also affect other people's lives because they radiate out to the person we're thinking of. We cannot see it-but it proves itself at times when two people have the same thought, spontaneously.

Remember, thoughts are waves of motion, a vibration, a whirling vortex of electrical energy that travels at about the speed of light.

Thoughts are the <u>weavers</u> of light. Their patterns are woven into a form by the exchange of energy between the two electric workers of positive and negative electricity, which is created by the friction of the motion as they exchange energy with each other. It's a pumping motion.

There are bands of thought waves, much like layers of clouds, only invisible, recorded in the gases, that drift through space, and in passing can influence your mind; that is why it is important to watch what kind of thoughts you keep company with.

These thought waves-bad or good-have been put there by humans like you and me, and affect all other humans. If we are in a bad mood-it is compounded by other negative thoughts from space-like attracts like-where your thoughts are, you are there.

What type of vibrations are you attracting or contributing?

The late Nobel Prize Winning Scientist, George Feynman, explained that he could see the vibrations from Russia and other Countries in the invisible airwaves as they passed by, here in America. Some people have this type of vision, like radar. He said, "It's really strange."

We are all heading for this kind of Awareness. It is part of our New Age of Man development-one of our many newly added attractions.

We are heading for a world where, in thought as well as by telegraph and plane, we will touch many parts of the invisible as well as the visible world. Some people can already do this-it's the higher <u>mental</u> world into which man has been moving and it is said, that is why there are many people with mental problems at this time.

We function on a physical, emotional and mental level, and in the transition from the <u>emotional</u> aspect of the personality to the <u>mental</u> thought – world of <u>mind</u>-we are learning how to control <u>thoughts</u>. This enables us to stabilize our emotions, which can toss us about like a ship on a wild sea.

Controlling and directing these thoughts is part of our goal.

Can you imagine anyone creating anything worthwhile when in a constant state of turmoil?

Like a mischievous puppy, the mind <u>must</u> be brought under orderly control.

Beautiful thoughts create beauty as proven by people who took L.S.D. and other drugs. It was told to me, that under their influence-as they released their emotional problems, the moment the thought was ugly or beautiful-so was the face.

You were born beautiful-how are you doing now? Your <u>now</u> face is the result of years of your thoughts being imprinted on it by you. Watching faces is a great boost for thought control.

Thoughts are the tools used to create not only the body you wear-but all else in your life-including your children-it all started with a thought.

We now finish our explanation of thoughts and move on to the gasses.

Thoughts are light-wave pictures that are imprinted on the negative invisible gases which fill all space; they surround, separate, and record the pattern for each living body, as well as plants, animals and suns, keeping them in their own wave-fields as they float in this gaseous mist called space.

Like a beehive, God's body is the entire Light-wave Universe, with each one of us living in it-within his own Cubicle of Light.

There are nine invisible inert gases, so named because of their passivity and fluidness. Their home is in the <u>Still Center</u> of every animate object, the eye of the tornado, seed of a plant, center of a planet or centering man. Their names you will find on the Chart of the Elements in Science, the first and last are called, Alpha and Omega.

Does that ring a bell in your mind?

Jesus said, "I am the Alpha and Omega," meaning the beginning and the end, the Circle of Completeness.

He had completed His earthly journey and was <u>aware</u> of it. He knew the Secrets of the Universe, which are the <u>Laws of How It Works</u>-The reason He could walk on water and perform Miracles, and left his Word to be proven by Science hundreds of years later.

He was the first one to overcome the urges of the Cell body and was in total <u>command</u> of the Super-Conscious Mind; He had become One with the All-Knowing Mind of God.

His purpose on earth was to show <u>us</u> how to do it-to set the Pattern.

He said: "Follow Me."

Isn't it exciting to know Science has used the same names for these two gases, Alpha and Omega, as mentioned in the Bible?

It is said, Science and Religion will some day unite. The two equal opposites, each complimenting and proving the other, the thinking and feeling aspects of life, which at present, are a bit at odds with each other.

These Cosmic gases are the Seed Patterns of the Universal Mind's dream, that give order and form to your creations, the same gases that moved upon the face of the waters at the time of Creation.

If they could speak they might say something like this:

"I am your Personal Genii, you may ask for anything you desire and I will bring it to you, shaped as your thoughts created it-in your image and likeness-to bring you Joy or Sorrow----for----"

"I am the Slumbering Spiritual Giant within you that brings all things into being."

These wonderful gases are pumped into your body by your breath and circulated throughout your skeleton in the form of a gaseous substance in the blood, where it receives and records any meaningful, thoughts, emotions, memories, or adjustments you may make in the pattern of your mind or body during your lifetime.

As in the seed of any plant or tree, these gases form the Seed-Idea of you from which you are born.
So there you are, Eternally recorded in space, to be re-run in another lifetime, in another body, which

you have re-patterned <u>yourself</u> in the seed of the inert gases.

As a child you may have heard your parents say-"God knows everything you do"-or some have called it the Recording Angel that keeps track of all your sins-well, this is <u>IT</u>. This is how God knows <u>all things</u>. This is God's Bookkeeping System.

Are you satisfied with what you are recording? Would you like to re-run it all again? The patterns remain just as they are until <u>you</u> change them by changing your thoughts and actions – your ways of living.

Through this recording system of gases-God keeps His Universe in perfect Balance-each reaps his own rewards and pays his own debts-no one to bail you out-no one to blame but <u>you</u> **<u>RESPONSIBILITY</u>**.

Now we will go behind the scenes and see how this Intelligence works <u>inside</u> the cells.

Inside each cell of your body is a basic coil of Atoms and Molecules, genes, etc., and the basic <u>D.N.A.</u>, which carries the building code for every part of your body just as a Carpenter, has a complete set of plans to build a house. <u>D.N.A.</u> is the Master Builder of the body through which the cosmic gases work.

When we go inside the cells, we are moving from gases to solids. They do not mix for if they did, no forms could be built.

So-the gases which are the Spirit working through the body, carrying your seed pattern, directed by the D.N.A. code, which directs the activities of all the cells as they group to build your organs; heart, lungs, kidneys, etc., which when formed are held in shape by the gases-somewhat like Jell-O in a mold.

These gases exert a 15 pound pressure per square inch around the entire earth as well as your body-you would fly off into space if this were not so. This pressure is called Gravity.

Gravity is the effect of the pumping action set up by the two spiraling forces of positive and negative motion of light-waves-as they interchange with each other to obey God's and your desires to create.

An accordian is a good example-it has to be pumped to produce music; the pumping pressure creates light-waves of motion, which you cannot see, but we can hear the music it produces.

Here we will say a word about the Cosmic Pump.

Our Sun is the Great Cosmic Pump in the Heavens from which the Breath of God radiates our

Seed Patterns in the form of the Inert Gases to give birth to all Life on earth.

Remember-Jesus prayed-"Our Father who Art in Heaven."

As each animate object is born, it is centered by a pumping action and breathes at it's own rate of speed-momentum, just as a body is given life and breathes through the Mother. Then after birth has its own pulse-beat centered in the heart. It is then beating with the Universal heartbeat on its own.

The earth's heartbeat is centered at the Equator.

We will now return to the gases.

Between D.N.A. and these gases is the sheerest film of viscous substance, giving D.N.A. the closest point of contact of working with the Spirit-it's the Spirit's-Right-hand-man.

Now we have a body of cells with the Spirit in the form of gases coursing through our blood stream, designed originally in God's perfect pattern, altered by our own thoughts, desires and ways of living, and our genetic pattern which we have earned through the law of attraction.

Can you see how you have made your body what it is today, and that you can never be separated from God, and why it is called the Temple of God?

There are many Bible Verses to substantiate this, quote:

"I in you, you in Me and both of us one in the Father," Jesus said.

"Nearer than hands and feet."

And as to the recording gases; "Each hair of your head is numbered."

"Not a sparrow falleth that I know not of."

We are ever so softly nestled in the Bosom of our Loving Creator.

* * * *

3
Cells – Our Garment of Protection

Welcome now to this wonderful body of cells in which we live, also known as the Genetic Entity, has taken billions of years to perfect, nine months to build and can be destroyed in an instant!

There are about 433 billion cells that make up your body. They are in a constant state of terrific motion, renewing themselves immediately as they die by the two-way interchange of positive and negative electrical energy, death giving birth to life.

Dr. Russell showed us a piece of Radium encased in a glass tube. In the dark you could see the "dying" sparks of light flashing from it. He said-"This is what death is-energy being released from your body in flashes of light," which record on the invisible film of space (the gases), the Pattern for the renewal of your body-just as a picture you take must have a negative from which it is developed.

What we call death is just being invisible to people in cell bodies: some people call them ghosts when seen. The reason it is invisible is that the cells are depolarized or dead, just as your battery is dead when the energy is completely used, as our energy is also used after a period of time; we alternate

29

between being visible and invisible. Like Casper the friendly ghost we are in a dimension where we are free to move about as quickly as a thought-no cells to bind us.

Like an hour-glass, one half filled with sand which trickles into the lower empty half-then reverses to repeat the action, we too are sifted by life from a state of visible motion to a state of invisible rest-to be reversed when we have been recharged through that rest to inhabit another cell body.

This interchange has been going on for millions of years-but some of us are just now finding out about it. It will continue indefinitely until all beings have learned to live in peace and harmony with each other, "That is the Play." Then-that Peace on Earth will take place as promised-but you are a part of Creating that peace. This is how we are co-creators with God. This is the purpose of creation.

How long do we have to wait?

It depends on everyone's effort.

Start Today!

To continue:

Cells are transparent globules of light compressed into a form by the pressure of gravity and the inert gases, the invisible part of God's body, which fills all space. Like us, God has a visible and invisible body.

The visible and the invisible work together as a father and mother do to create their children. We are pumped from the darkness of space, the womb, into this world of light by the breath of God to which we are connected; we inhale at birth and as we leave this earth the breath is withdrawn-exhaled. You might say our pump is worn out.

The breath of God in our Solar System is the pumping action between our Sun and Earth. Father Sun and Mother earth are the Cosmic Lovers that started this dream of Creation in the gaseous space of the heavens. Their two wave-fields can be seen through a telescope, their misty arms reaching out to join each other in their Cosmic Mating dance in Space.

There are two kinds of cells. First, the egg and sperm cells, which never die, they are called germ cells, they unite when mating takes place, and are the initial impulse for the mechanism of building cell bodies. They came to life in the first seed atoms that were radiated from the Sun and imbedded in the ocean's waters-the Patterned Seed Atoms for bodies, to be wrapped within its earthly cloak of minerals and chemicals to become visible. They are passed along from one generation to another for the continuation of genetic cell bodies--- the Human Race.

The main reason to know you can never die is that you are Eternally recorded in your Personal Seed Atom in Space!

We are the product of these seed-sperm cells-these were our beginnings from the first Seed-Idea in the mind of the Creator as He dreamed of His Creation. As our dear Teacher said: "You were with me before the worlds were formed-before the beginning of time."

Then secondly there are the somatic cells that form everything that has to do with visible bodies, referred to in Genesis as-the dust of the earth-the chemicals.

**One theory is that at a certain time in cell development, some cells became multi-cellular and started specializing in developing structures-which later became known as Soma cells, of which our bodies are made. The purpose of this cell body is that God may enjoy his Creation in Action, just as we enjoy our family that is no longer just a dream. You might say cells are God's Ultimate of Creation at this point in time. Because of them we can communicate, feel and hold each other in a loving embrace as a solid object.

We are God's earthly garden of Creatures over whom He watches carefully, and Jesus did pray-"Our Father who art in Heaven" and we refer to the earth as Mother. The body is a precious tool to be used for the highest purpose.

How we have abused it! Not without serious consequences.

A cell remembers its code in the D.N.A. molecules and develops perfectly if not interfered with. What we do or do not put into the body affects each cell.

Under the direction of D.N.A., a cell builds all the organs of and in the body, and chooses the proper nourishment from the food we eat to nourish each cell and organ-also for it's repair and function. Each organ requires <u>some</u> different types of food to keep healthy-the reason for a well balanced diet.

A cell will respond to your attention-remember-it has a Center of Intelligence-and can eventually bring itself to total health if conditions are corrected that are harmful to it's survival; which is-proper food-rest-good emotions-lots of love-the greatest healer.

It has the ability to combine with other cells to carry out it's function as a group-the organs-heart and other parts of the body.

Cells become a solid mass of cooperative Intelligent action-such as building a body under the control of <u>instinct</u>, automatically after conception.

<u>Instinct</u> is an electrical impulse of patterns used by the Creator to control His Universe until man's

own consciousness unfolds in Awareness, enabling him to think and be able to control his own life,

A body of cells can live in suspended animation indefinitely, as proven by Yogis of India, who were buried alive; can also be kept alive on a life support system for years, even though the Spirit is mostly withdrawn from it.

A cells structure consist of atoms, molecules, protons, neutrons and other components-proteins-amino acids, etc. all spiraling around a black hole of Still Magnetic invisible Light, from which it's motion began and to which it returns as it's cycle of energy is completed.

And you, my dears, are the Spiritual Being centering a group of these Cosmic Cells called a Human Body. How well are you doing with yours? And as with one late famous General we reiterate---

"I SHALL RETURN"

**See Acid and Alkaline by Herman Aihara

4
The Elephant

White watching a T.V. program on "Training Wild Elephants in the Jungles of Africa" to work for humans, I became intensely aware of the how and why, over eons of time the Cosmic Cell has been transmuted through its many stages before it became useable in a human body.

His bulky right hind leg tied to a huge tree trunk in the jungle, by a thick, long, heavily knotted rope – the rebellious, trumpeting elephant was first lashed, then patted and a kind word spoken to it occasionally by its Trainer, as its' will defied being submissive to a Power greater than its own.

As it tugged violently to free itself – it fell exhausted to the ground several times – then up again! to protest losing its freedom – each time becoming more gentle and teachable until at last, it surrendered to be yoked – for service-to his new life of hauling the felled trees of the jungle.

Through this Training, the cells and the will of the Elephant had Surrendered to Obedience, and that new memory was then recorded over the old cell memory of the elephant's body pattern, as well as the electric pattern in the seed gases. These will in turn be handed down through the genes for repetition in its offspring, eventually breeding a more gentle domesticated line of elephants. All of our domesticated animals, as well as man, have at sometime been cultivated in a similar manner, from instinct to "Awareness of Action." Pain seems to be the basic element needed for change – making them and us more Aware.

How like the Human Family it sounds, the parents' training and guiding the children and themselves to overcome and redirect their negative emotional attitudes and patterns, all obeying, in some way, a power greater than their own; the children to the parents, (hopefully), the cats and dogs to the family rules. We obey the rules of schools, neighborhoods, and cities, then there are State and world laws to be obeyed, until at last we are ready to make the greatest surrender of all, to the will of our Creator. As a Human Family, we are all working together to bring Unity to a many-patterned world – at times knowingly, but <u>always</u> instinctively.

That very night I came to understand <u>how</u> and <u>why</u>, Reincarnation is really the Transmutation of the Cosmic Cell through the ever-growing Awareness of the Consciousness.

Bodies of cells born, reborn, reshaped, recombined, and refined through billions of years. Always – new memories are being impressed over old ones, the old ones filed away as the instinctive memories and habit patterns of today's highly refined minds and bodies of man. All of this is recorded in the INERT GASSES. - - **Our History**.

* * * *

5
A Nod To The Dinosaurs

There was a period of time when huge thick-skinned, heavy bodied, monstrous looking animals roamed our earth – for a period longer than any other living thing. Some of these Dinosaurs had heavily plated armor, spiked with saw-toothed edges along their horny spines, some with spiked heads, and others with a ball of spikes at the end of their dog-like tails; all were suited to defend themselves against the notorious meat-eater, Tyrannosaurus Rex, they call him, The most ferocious of all the Dinosaurs – 360 sharp teeth in double rows lined its wide mouth, waiting to tear apart any creature he could eat! What battles must have raged in those lush green jungles as the long-necked, Vegetarian defended itself from T. Rex; two beasts, tails thrashing amid howls of pain, each nearly two stories high we hear, caught in a struggle for life. The long neck of the Brontosaurus is said to have developed over long periods of time from reaching high into the air for its food, after it ran for safety into the nearby waters.

Then picture the huge bat-winged Flying Pterodactyl whose sharply clawed feet dug deep into the hillside as it climbed to find a higher plateau, to give impetus to its heavy body when it wanted to fly. Its broad wingspan of nearly six feet – holding aloft its Dracula-like form as it coasted over the tall trees and ferns below. We wonder –

was it searching for food – or just out for a fast spin? - - - It boggled our imaginations when we heard of these strange creatures! All day long they foraged for the hundreds of pounds of food a day needed to keep their huge bodies alive. There has been some conjecturing as to whether those ancient creatures are the ancestors of our present day birds, the way in which the joints of the feet and legs are assembled points to the greatest number of facts that say – yes.

All of this and perhaps much more was taking place on Young Mother Earth as it circled spit-like, closely around its parent Sun in the early days of its own Transformation. The coarser bodies of that time could withstand the intense light waves of the sun; those eventually decaying bodies that would be returned to earth, compressed, layer upon layer, then sealed between crusts of earth along with the foliage; to be digested into beds of coal, and pockets of oil, where the tale of life and death is molded into the strata's of rock imbedded deep within the earth, to be pried into later in time, by Paleontologists, Archeologists, and other-seekers of answers – for Why everything is as it is. Those bodies that were kneaded into the earth through alternating Cataclysms of Ice Ages and Tropical Eras that renewed the earth by raising up new areas of continents and submerging the worn out parts into its seas, to reshuffle its treasures for new generations of Races, who will in turn, search for our story in the rocks.

The Eternal see-saw of <u>Balance</u> through periods of time, <u>Transform</u> – <u>Transmute</u> – and <u>Transfigure</u> – the three important big T's of History; their effects can be seen throughout the world each day of our lives – ever moving us forward and up.

* * * *

6
And Now Man
Our Amazing Ancestors

The Age of the Caveman now breaks its news to the world! We picture them as chomping away on the raw meat of a wild animals leg, not only ingesting its cells, but also having some of the wild animal's <u>memory</u> in the make-up of their very own body cells; as we imagine them to be, their shaggy haired cumbersome bodies slightly bent forward with deep-set eyes peering from under wild thatches of matted hair – carrying clubs. A far cry from our present day concept of Adam and Eve as the first Creatures created. Today our clubs are more refined, polished, well shaped – but just as forceful, however, and we nibble instead, daintily, on a roasted chicken or turkey leg. The hair is well styled and sprayed – up to the tune of all most two hundred dollars! Bombs that work much faster than clubs – slay whole races and the land as well. But as the old saying goes – the proof of the pudding is in the eating, and our proof is the remains of human skeletons – found – exhumed, and pieced together to testify to the Origin of Man and his many <u>stages of development</u> through <u>long</u> periods of time. Might we then suppose the Seven Days of Creation – are those Periods of Time it took to evolve to the Creation of man—And then came Adam? - -How do we enumerate these periods in comparing them with the Biblical version of Creation?

On through time again we move, and we find the cell bodies much more under the control of man's awareness, for we now have Fire – and the meat is roasted. Another step forward in cell refinement and <u>Consciousness</u>.

Perhaps a few thousand or million years later down the line, the vegetarians and fruit-eaters arrive on the scene. By now we have spiraled still farther from the Sun, and bodies are losing much of their wild hairy appearance. These are all Transformations under the instinctive guidance of the Spirit within man, showing the diversity of Nature's body-building processes for refining the cells as the Human Race evolves – each Group expressing its own life-styles according to the Evolution of the Consciousness for <u>that</u> period of time.

But - - when the Sowers and Reapers brought Agriculture to the Human Race – it is said to have been the <u>greatest</u> step forward; now we have natural whole grains of wheat pounded into flour for the Bread of Life – and eventually other grains in many forms – corn – rye – oats – barley – and many others, all said to be the <u>basis</u> for good health even to this very day, by our New Age Holistic Doctors and other Good-Health Researchers. Why? Because of their rich source of B-Vitamins found in few other foods – the Complete B Complex, B-1 through B-12 – all needed to keep the vital energy coursing through our bodies, calm nerves, the gray from your hair and unlined skin, a good pick-up in place of coffee and other refreshers which rob our body of these <u>daily</u> needed Vitamins, for they are not retained longer, as are some others.

Our store shelves are lined with a large variety of these grains – a few are still all natural – most others are refined and sugared, a drawback to our good health of today.

Their birth in time is believed to have come about 10,000 years ago with the Stone Age Man; the last remnant of their tribes were found as late as 1930 by Naturalist-Scientists; Probing deep into the heart of New Guinea jungles and Rain Forests, they found thousands of them in separate Tribes carrying on their Stone Age Traditions – still with bones in their noses, and wielding hand made weapons (like poles) which were used for warring as well as farming, and wearing Bird-of-Paradise-feathered head-dresses, in which they believed their Ancestors' Spirits came to live. Their bodies seem to be in much better condition than some of our modern day bodies – with the exception of Teeth – Dentists – a blessing of our time.

On sloping hills, one could see for miles, gardens of food in perfectly squared plots, looking much like our Western farms. *Sweet Potatoes were one of their main crops, which were dug from the ground by hand, by women, at harvesting time along with a large variety of fruits picked from many types of Palm Trees. They paid their debts with choice pigs after losing a battle. The pigs were mainly tended by the women even to sleeping in their huts while the men slept in separate groups, for they feared by mixing with the women too much they would lose their aggressiveness and manhood. Food for thought.

Today women have infiltrated almost everywhere a man has had some privacy! It's too early to tell what this change is leading to or what the results will be. Is it any wonder some men feel frustrated and displaced?

And alas! The airplane has brought Civilization to Primitive Man's ways – the clothing has changed somewhat – due to the Missionaries, the young people are torn between two worlds – the old and the new ways. In modern style, they now have their fruits and vegetables displayed for sale at out-door markets and use a type of paper money.

Can you imagine the changes taking place in the Consciousness of these Native peoples that until 1930 had never been photographed nor seen a white man? On hearing an old fashioned, hand-wound phonograph they thought the voices were Spirits – so to keep them under control the Explorers used gunfire by shooting an animal. All those new memories were being registered in their body cells and Consciousness – we may be seeing how some of our very own beginning changes came about. New skills will be added as the old ones become memories – all Patterned by Nature, the Great Transformer!

*See the story of Dr. George Washington Carver about the miracles of the sweet potato's use in today's world, in the booklet "The Man Who Talks With The Flowers" by Glenn Clark – Macalaster Publishing Co.

7
Today's World

Shall we now take our greatest leap in time and arrive at what we know today as the Industrial or Machine Age – and the age of Robots, Radio, Radar, Television, Computers, Atomic Subs, and Atom Bombs – all are well documented on T.V. and in the newspapers? The age of speed – work faster, produce more, prosperity for everyone, implanting new skills into already wearied and driven bodies, to be extended to other bodies and minds to carry forward to the even greater inventions of the outer Space Age (no time to contact Inner Space) where, from the Voyager out among the Stars, we see our own Mother Earth, hung like a blue opalescent jewel, glowing against the darkness of space.

But given a closer look reveals to us the records of its slow destruction from oil spills and pollution, for threaded throughout parts of its turquoise ocean waters are patches of ugly greenish brown waste. A mature Mother Earth now seasoned and scarred from the experience of being drilled and dug into by huge man-made machines for its pre-historic treasures of oil, coal, and minerals to supply energy and heat for new and finer bodies that wear clothes instead of hair – but eat just as voraciously as did the Dinosaurs – a Restaurant on nearly every corner to keep alive the Story of Man; her forests mercilessly hacked and sawed to death for our out of control population – never mind that trees are needed for Earths Balance – why think of tomorrow – do as you please – still unaware of this holy Law of Balance. Tomorrow will take care of itself – and it does, with jobless homeless people living under bridges, in cars with their children – foraging in bins of discarded food in back of stores. Some of these humans, sick and confused trudging to Soup Kitchens for handouts, at the mercy of our contributions to help them survive.

Some others of these same bodies that helped usher in this new age of change – are discarded like on old pair of shoes – homes, savings, and pensions lost as businesses move to other parts of the world to make more dollars, leaving behind a trail of disaster worse than a Tornado, while rows of vacant store windows gape at us block after block – like rows of mournful hollow masks – as we drive the Avenue. Decadence on display!

Questions hang like weights upon our minds. Sometimes Life seems to crush us in its mad turmoil as it rushes on the way to its fulfillment.

To find the answer isn't easy.

In searching through the history of world changes we find, that when a New Stage in Man's development is about to be born, there is always great confusion, even wars as the Transformation takes place – in the world as well as in our own personal lives.   We are all being processed to

Perfection by the Creator as we circle around our Great Father Sun.

The Natives in the Jungle tho' invaded peacefully this time by the white man – never-the-less, it disturbed their way of life – Nature's urgent call to move forward. We are also being invaded overwhelmingly by immigrants, refugees, and illegal persons – all because of the desire to be free in soul and body. We of the older generation have made our adjustments through great trials – theirs are only beginning. Some are disappointed (did they expect heaven on earth?); still others greedily take all they can get, while others are very appreciative of this new privilege. Does their attitude depend on how much suffering was left behind?

The confusion is partly caused by not understanding the purpose of life – its laws and our place in the scheme of things, in some ways we are still like children in our understanding; and while knowing this doesn't eliminate all the suffering, it might be comforting to know that it is the Law of Balance at work – the Savior of Mankind these pairs of opposites – because they let us know, loudly, when we have gone to far to the left or right – with a warning – like a sharp rap to the knuckles – we'd better change before it is too late! If we haven't learned from previous mistakes, the story repeats itself on other levels 'till we do. Pain seems to leave the biggest impression for turning our lives around.

In our grasping for things we have become caught up with the images and hustled along with the crowd, given up our Authority to the Government, T.V., Doctors, Drugs, and Promiscuousness and what the world thinks, instead of finding out the Truth for ourselves. Do you remember what the Truth is? --

That you are created in the Image and Likeness of God! - -instead we've imaged ourselves in terms of dollars, T.V. heroes, Movie Stars, and other false gods. It's time we take back our Authority and follow the True Image. "Thou shalt have no false gods before Me."

But - - underneath all this turmoil and confusion – for sometime now – silently – almost stealthily, there has been a deep low rumbling in the bosom of Mother Earth, not unlike a huge giant that has been chained by those who would separate the Creator from His Creation; a Giant whose mighty muscles are being flexed throughout the world for the Count-down that will determine the future of mankind – the Spirit of Love – inviting all those who are willing to share in bringing forth this great New Age that has been bursting itself into the world for nearly two thousand years – the Giant for the Will of the Universe – **"LOVE YE ONE ANOTHER"** – THE BROTHERHOOD OF MAN.

Can we make it this time?

8
The Eyes of God
The Invisible Side of Life

Just as the planets spin on their axis with a North and South pole – we, too, are positioned in space with an invisible axis, - The North Pole at our head and South Pole at our feet – Science calls them Poles of Rotation; we use the term, Eyes of God, because these two Forces of Energy which are projected into space along with the East and West poles (termed here the Arms of God) by the Creator at the moment of your conception, measures out your personal invisible energy field, just as you would measure plans for the foundation of a house or garden plot, to form a Cube of Light in which the personal seed atom for building your body is centered. That same seed atom of energy that was impelled to struggle upward through the dark tube tunnel to imbed itself in the mother's egg to become a body identified as <u>you</u>. It carries the complete record of your body's history of development through the ages, plus the present plans to become the fine instrument it is today, functioning instinctively with little training, to free us for adding new abilities as well as to develop greater <u>mental</u> capacities. This is the Age of Mental Achievements that has carried us into the Budding Age of Man to further his Spiritual Climb.

These Cube Boundaries are the Laws of Limitation set up by the Creator to Balance the <u>free</u>

51

<u>will</u> He would give to us, allowing us to go so far and no farther at this time.

Standing at the Center of your Cube World, you are the Actor in this Play as well as its Creator; this is the home of the Pairs of Opposites in your every day life that you must learn to balance and keep in harmony with God's laws if you want a peaceful and happy life. This is where the most important transition takes place, being that the individual is the <u>Basis</u> for the whole of Creation.

This Cube of Light World has been described by Dr. Russell as the Mirrors of Infinity. For being six-sided they multiply and reflect back to you exactly what you are creating just as your mirror reflects back to you your image as you stand before it. So – what you want in your life you must first learn to <u>give</u> and be – for only what you <u>give</u> can be multiplied – happy or unhappy – good or evil. Think about this – if God pronounced His Creation as all <u>good</u> – what is evil? All the evil in the world is born from someone's mistaken decision," and it has been so since the beginning of man.

Does this explain to you the meaning of Jesus' "Do unto others as you would have them do unto you?" or "As you sow so shall you reap?" Your actions not only reflect what your inner thoughts are like, they also reflect to others and influence them, for "By their acts ye shall know them."

With a little better understanding of how our invisible home works – we know <u>why</u> certain things happen in our lives, broken friendships, lack of love, successes or failures – it usually begins with us.

How to correct these problems? The Scales of Balance come to us at this point – try doing exactly the <u>opposite</u> of what you have been doing until the problem area (like the opposite side of the scale) or what you want, starts manifesting or comes into balance. It's that simple.

Friends? Give true friendship, and try loving people in spite of their faults. More money? Give to others wisely, the hungry and/or children's groups, etc. Better job or promotion? – Give your all with Love, not just for a payday. <u>Service</u> is the answer. Give to Life your all, lovingly and willingly, knowing that your six-sided Mirrors of Light are returning them to you <u>multiplied.</u> It takes some <u>practice</u> and <u>patience</u>, but the results will someday surprise you! This is simple basic Therapy that can be done in the privacy of your own home at no expense, and builds the bridge between you ant the Spirit within.

Because we are all in this Game of Life together, there are a few Rules to be followed, and for those who have forgotten or not heard of them; that Man of Wisdom, Jesus, came to rescue us from our earthly dilemma (forgetting our True purpose in life): set the example; and gave a few simple

Guidelines in the Sermon on the Mount, and if practiced the Eight Beatitudes to tell of their fulfillment; plus His many admonitions to those who followed Him, as recorded in the Gospels – "Your sins are forgiven thee – go – and sin no more" (change your ways); and as every game has a Goal – our Goal is Liberation – from what? From the false idea that you are a physical body subject to all evils, instead of a Spiritual Being in <u>charge</u> of a physical body. This body of Atomic cells is the God created material we were given at birth to transmute until the Inner Light glows through them as the Sun shines through a clear glass window. Artists depict this Light as Halos around Jesus, and other spiritually dedicated Beings. Today we have our Albert Schwietzers, Mother Theresas, and many of whom we never hear, but they exist as the silent workers. The Saints caught the message He gave, and though many of them led lives of not too good an example, when they caught the Vision – they turned their lives around and became dedicated to serving humanity. By their example they continued to preserve the Message of Christ who left us with these rewarding words, "In my Fathers House are many Mansions, I go to prepare a place for you." He left to us in His stead the Inner Voice of the Holy Spirit to guide us. This Voice acts as Intuition (the 6th sense), or as symbols in dreams as Joseph had of the seven lean and the seven fat ears of corn, then later at times it becomes audible. It's the Inner Magnet that has been with us since the beginning of time, but we had lost contact. Now, because of His Powerful Presence, it has re-awakened and keeps drawing us back into balance. We must listen carefully to become aware of those urges within to keep from losing our way; and because all of Creation is made-up of a vibration of Light waves of energy, upon His death the Power from His Atomic Body structure and Consciousness permeated the earth causing the earthquakes at that time. It also permeated the Souls of His Followers and those who were ready, and they became conductors for passing on this Holy Energy to others through their works. Being aware of this connects us, "tunes us in." Our body is our own Special Tool, a group of Spirit centered Atoms that conduct this energy to others to the extent we are aware of and use it – through prayer or works. This infused energy is the power that transmutes the cells and consciousness and as science has noted; we inhale these invisible Atoms from many beings, who have long ago left the earth, as they are recycled in their Journey through Space. Who knows what famous Atoms are inspiring us – perhaps even some from Jesus, as one well known lecturer suggested.

We have many choices and opportunities, plus free will and a lifetime or more in which to complete them: like a tree that is staked and fed when planted to keep it growing straight and strong – we need these Guidelines; not that a twisted and gnarled tree trunk isn't a thing of beauty because of having taken the Circuitous Path, - but that in taking too many detours – we might waste our energy and time before we reach our goal. Nevertheless, how we find God matters little – only that we <u>find</u> Him, but might it not be easier to arrive in one whole piece?

At one time also it seemed necessary to enter a Monastery or Nunnery to find this Inner Peace and Love – and it <u>was</u> for that period of time – because through their dedication we derived our Holy Ones and Sages, the Wayshowers who built the Foundation that brought the new extension of Consciousness to be the impetus for moving humanity forward <u>again</u> in its climb to perfection. Out of the Dark and Middle Ages came these saints and we are the results of their efforts – the present day Footstools for holding the Balance of Consciousness. Heaven knows we need it in today's world. Thus does Creation ever move forward – and e'en though it seems to fall – like the waves of the Ocean, ever at ebb and flo, bringing newly washed sands upon the beach – so are we the Waves of Consciousness, bringing fresh new levels of Awareness to our ever troubled world.

This all unfolds rather slowly, it seems, but too much power without intelligent control can be devastating as our observations will tell us – we seem still to be at the "Teenage stages of Consciousness."

Also during that period of time some seekers thought it necessary to flagellate and cover the body with sackcloth and ashes to purify it for its misdeeds; today we know it is the mind (mental) that is the Intruder (double-faced – positive and negative)-it's the Dragon that must be slain at the door before we can enter the Secret place of the Most High, the home where our True Self resides. Fairy Tales as well as the Bible are filled with symbols of <u>how</u> this Search is enacted within man's Consciousness. For one – the Prince slays the Dragon and rescues the Princess from the Palace dungeon (the mortal mind), the slayer of the Real. How? It argues, defies, disputes, rebels, rationalizes, falsifies, blames, judges, and procrastinates, and uses many other tricks (it's the real devil), to keep us from finding the Babe in the Manger – the Budding True Self of us – symbolized by the Princess. The Prince, of course, is the Spirit of Love and Life within us as it struggles to hold its Balance as we go through our daily trials of the human will, until we finally surrender to the Divine. We cannot enter this Holy of Holies with an unleavened mind; it would destroy us and others with its negative power, as we also see in the world, power without Compassion. We become wise enough through these trials to at last outwit this misguided human mind and are allowed, even <u>invited</u> to enter our True Home once again. This inner yearning for something we know not what – is finally fulfilled. A Peace comes upon us, the Intellect (head) and the heart (feelings) are sparring partners that at last have become a Balanced Pair – in Harmony with the Whole; equal and opposite created He them, the female carrying the light and the male caring for her. We must always use <u>some</u> reasoning (male) to determine the correctness of our feelings (female) in order to stabilize and harmonize them.

You can see then why the body is important – it is the place of mediation between the Soul and God, and upon it is transcribed the results of our thoughts and emotions. If we don't concede willingly to change, Nature will find a way to persuade us. <u>Pressure</u> is the force that <u>causes</u> all things to be transmuted, where there is a pressure there is a need for change or action of some kind.

Those Tellers of Tales were aware of mans' struggle to overcome, and relayed it in beautifully told Fables and Stories of Life, which also give us clues in secret ways for its solution; our work is to become Aware of them. God speaks to us from <u>everything</u> in life.

Today we have many tools to help clear these impeding opposites, but there must be consent and willingness – openness to change.

Then came new methods of help in the guise of Psychology, with Wilhelm Reich's strange phone booth – like Cabinet experiments, who was supposed to be the first to discover the measurable quantity of the Soul as it left the body and it was grossly condemned by supposed authorities; then came Carl Jung, the first of them to include the Soul as the <u>basis</u> for all his analysis, which also raised eyebrows; but we can't care about raised eyebrows whenever the Inner conviction comes, we <u>must</u>

obey, as the Creator keeps His Creation ever renewed for progress through new understanding. And just who raises those eyebrows to judge? Of course it's the invading Intellect (the doubting Thomas of the Scripture, the Dragon at the Door of the Mind). Since then many other types of therapy have evolved to become almost a science.

Psychosomatic Medicine at first gingerly raised its head to be followed by many others too numerous to mention here. Now we have Holistic doctors with the idea of bringing Mind and Body together to prevent rather than treat effects, with many wonderful results: but the ideal we are working toward is the integrating of Mind, Body, and Soul, with Spirit ever being asked to join to show us the way – the Unified Field – our Being made Whole once again. It takes all of the make-up of man to function in Rhythm and Harmony with the Whole. This is true Evolution and Transmutation – it's the only purpose of Life; the Spirit moving freely through all of Nature, the mind and body, prevents and removes the crystallized belief structures that have been built around false man-made ideas, the obstacles the Prince clears away with this Sword of Truth to rescue the Princess and restore to life the sleeping (unaware areas) household of the Palace – our True Home Within. And with our Beloved Teacher who said: "I have overcome the World," we too can add our efforts and successes to promote truth.

Our Holy Book Says,

"I will instruct thee and teach thee in the way which thou shalt go: I will guide thee with mine eye."

Psalm 32:8

* * * *

MAKE HASTE!

O Exquisiteness of GOD – How you hold all
Things in your loving hands—waiting to
Express your Light through each one.

Make Haste, you idlers! Can't you see the
                    Goal ahead?
Must you dilly-dally here and there with
Foolishness when the precious fullness
Of life awaits you with open arms?

Make haste! Keep eyes on singleness of
purpose,
All else will fall away like dew before the
Morning sun. Heed not the things you see, but
Keep in mind the truth you know. Let this
Be your guideline, hold firmly to it, and it will
Lead you to your goal.

* * * *

9
Rhythm Is Our Business
The Wave, Timing and Cycles

Rhythm is our Mating Dance with Life - the way in which we flow with it, on finding it, we bring Harmony and Love into our life.

Rhythm means to flow freely with something – to be in accord with it – to sway gently to and fro – to follow in unison; it is a light wave of energy that passes throughout all of Nature and as it passes through our body, we use it as a Musician uses an instrument. It has its high and low points – the high is the peak, when you're at your <u>best</u> – and the low point is the ebbing – the withdrawing into yourself to recharge to move forward again. The secret of accomplishment is learning to use it to our advantage as it passes through us in our own personal wave cycle. At times these cycles can bring important changes into our lives if acted upon, and they may not present themselves again for a long period of time, another cycle; that's why it is so important to be well aware of the moment – lest it escape us.

To blend with it successfully requires awareness of Timing; when you feel at your best or peak, make important decisions and handle the most necessary projects at hand, then as it ebbs into its lull to gather momentum for the next high peak, the smaller tasks can be done – or a rest period taken before starting again. To know when you are at ebb means that you may become emotional, impatient, drop or bump into objects for your attention has scattered, a rest is needed.

Concentration is an important part of using this energy, as it is a <u>mental</u> effort to keep things going smoothly, a one-pointedness of mind toward a certain goal as we move through these cycles of change.

The emotions are captured by the body's muscles and held there until the muscles become relaxed; anger, though for a good cause is recorded in the body as aches and pain, along with other negative emotions, and because it is an invasion by a foreign element, the body warns us that something is wrong. If continued it steals our energy making us tired, lowering our immune system's resistance, and it is responsible for many diseases, as Researchers for good health have proven to be true. Every negative emotion has only one place to go unless diverted – it collapses onto the body. So Therapists often suggest pounding a pillow, taking a <u>brisk walk – even screaming</u> (be sure the windows are closed), or handling it with a sense of humor. Let go – changing the mental circuit diverts many negative reactions, so have at hand a positive statement or prayer to quickly feed the mind in these emergencies as what gets there first usually wins. Remember – this energy is our Spiritual Life Force, which we are learning to control; the body receives and distributes it, but our Mind is the Director. We determine the results by our thinking.

Choosing the wrong partner for marriage or business can be our ruin. The more we are at one in our thinking with someone; the more harmony results because our Rhythms are similar. Imagine dancing a Waltz with someone who can only Cha-Cha – or not dance at all!

Now apply this principle to your family and friends and you can see why it takes so long to attain National and World Peace, where there are so many different rhythms and diverse languages – the Tower of Babel. Perhaps some day there will be one general language that we all speak, at the same time retaining our own inherited one, so we can all function together in harmony and peace with understanding.

Rhythm and harmony cannot be forced – it must be understood and loved into being – starting with our own family, as again, World Peace starts with the individual. Always, effort is needed, but soon you will find you can be in harmony with many different rhythms without becoming negative, because your mind and emotions are now under your control, instead of them controlling you!

This brings to mind the time we dined at a Country Music Restaurant, where we saw a pair of unusually graceful dancers for whom everyone cleared the floor. Caught in their Rhythm, they danced separately, but as one person dancing with his own shadow; no matter how intricate the steps became – and they had many, they moved as one. They must have practiced for hours to reach such perfection. We regretted that the music ever stopped – a rare sight.

Then there was that special night at the Hollywood Bowl with the Finland Concert Orchestra, whose rhythmic blending of instruments with their bodies was so perfect that they suddenly appeared to be puppets with the music flowing through them – a sight I've never again witnessed. It takes you beyond time into another dimension where perfect harmony seems to exist.

Yes – Rhythm is a wave and has a beat, something we can feel, each in his own way and timing – some can hear its inner tone: it also has a color, and of these things are we comprised: Light, Color, Tone, and Rhythm, with Light and Love as the basis for all of this Grand Phenomena of Beauty swirling in through and about us, the name for it is the Aura, that oval shaped protective sheath of Love that surrounds our body in the center of our invisible Cube of Light home.

Nature too, has its interesting surprises in Rhythm. Coming home from a vacation trip at the quaint mountain town of Wrightwood, Ca., we excitedly stopped our car and watched as a puffy white cloud shaped like a Long Bearded Dwarf about three feet tall with arms outstretched, bouncing up and down, to and fro, doing his own dance among a group of boulders known as the Mormon Rocks, a few feet from the side of the road. Up into the air about two or three feet he danced, then down again, he seemed to be fastened to that certain space by a magnet – a Special Show if you're in time to catch it! It was still bouncing as we left – we wondered for how long, and would anyone else get to see it? A delightful scene, stored away in our book of memories.

Or—high in the heavens among the billowy, grayed storm clouds that passed overhead on a mid-winter day – flowing North, one in the shape of an Ancient Turbaned Old Man of Baghdad, floating lazily along on his Magic Carpet Cloud with his long beard swirling upward, as though following the North Star for direction. I sketched him from memory as best I could. All of these things are there for the taking if you're a sky watcher or nature lover. The more you love – the greater the choices!

Even inanimate objects like kitchen appliances have their tone and rhythm, and give off a humorous story if you're inclined that way. Yes – everything has a Rhythm and Timing – be aware of yours. To allow ourselves time to dream and become aware of these other dimensions of which we are an extension, refreshes our lives and renews our health, as health is not found in a doctors office but in our Balance with Life.

It is said that the long slow rolling ocean waves are fed from the deep-down currents and that a ship will list and roll with their rhythms, but it's the small choppy waves which are caused by surface winds that will toss and rock the ship about and can totally destroy it. This also describes our physical dilemma – as we have been likened unto ships on the "Ocean of Life," and we need that deep inner poise to carry us successfully over Life's choppy seas. Rest restores Balance and puts us in touch with that deep Inner Peace. What do <u>you</u> need to bring into balance?

The wind tells us of its Rhythm by the bent of the trees as they sway in its path, while at the corner of my garden, a plants leaves will whirl round and round in circles for hours like a Whirling Dervish, as the wind is channeled along the wall of the house. In a tornado's lightning and thunder, the trees and houses seem to cling to the earth for their lives – sometimes to no avail. Yet – lightning, wind, and rain all play their necessary Rhythms, circling around Mother Earth to keep it alive and well in spite of all man's seeming effort to do otherwise. The interplay of all of these Rhythms is what adds up to the "Earth's Symphony in Space."

As we evolve up this "Ladder of Consciousness" more of these wonderful surprises unfold to us – that's really what the Joy of Living is all about – Discovery! Why wait to get to Heaven when heaven can be experienced in many ways right where you are. It's in the quietness of life that we touch the Soul and God unfolds to us his Secrets of Nature and the Heavens.

"Let your mind be as an Empty Bowl – turned up."

* * * *

"O Soul of mine, if thou shouldst ask what I
want most –
T'would be that I may see deep into the heart of
Thee
And know that loving tenderness – that all
enfolding
Warmness that is you.

I behold thy face! The soul of me reflected that
I may
See the pureness dwelling there – ever giving –
seeking
But to please.

Eternity stands still – for the moment our lips
meet –
The stillness is complete.

O Soul of mine thy yearning is fulfilled."

10
The One Mind and Its Attributes

We have now arrived at the door of the One Mind – that Center of Stillness, all-Knowing and all Power, the Divine Director of Creation, Maker of Dreams, and when moving, is a whirling vortex of energy that gives birth to all that is ever being discovered by man – the Mind that Jesus called, "Father."

Behind the scenes stands this Director, silently watching and waiting for us to ask the where, how, and why of things; that Giver of Gifts in which endless Secrets are nested, the Great Parent Mind. It fills all space and is the thought substance (light, atoms, molecules, etc.) from which all things are made, and in which we live our daily lives, much like the Bees in their combed Hive. It is indestructible and no matter how negative we become, we can never escape Its' ever loving vigilance, "For I am a patient God."

Then there is the so-called human mind – our own personal reflected portion of this One Mind, allotted to each one since the first Adam; but by turning away from its Source, it became limited in its perception of life, wanting to make its own decisions (the human will) and in so doing lost some of its Wisdom, as it slowly drifted from its

Parent Source, just as children do when they grow to that independent, know it all age, only to find that when the problems arrive they return home for some of that old-fashioned Mom and Pop advice – not to mention the dollars! Then like the balancing arms of God (forgiveness) that extend to us when we have strayed from our Source, we reach out to them with love. This is the beginning of Wisdom, the willingness to change, which sometimes leads to a Rebirth and we concede to the Greater will – which sets in motion the Transformation.

It is the small daily concessions to this Will that takes us into wider Vistas of Awareness, until the day we come into a balance that reaches neither too far to the left nor right, but beats its rhythm in tune with this Universal Harmony and the Transmutation is on its way. Through the Soul (feelings) this Mind speaks to us, and tho' it confers no special privileges to certain ones – to receive this gift we must make the effort of turning our attention to, and developing a relationship with it – the Divine Romance between the Soul and God, of which the Great Ones Speak.

Albert Einstein once commented, that when he wanted an answer to a mathematical equation on which he was working, he concentrated on every detail he could think of concerning it, then put it aside and went for a walk in the woods. At some time the answer would come to him. From where? This All-Knowing Mind, of course! Most of our great men have a reverence for this invisible

Intelligence, and tell of how it has presented answers in unique ways, via dreams and symbols, to their inquiries.

Practice is the key to building the bridge to it until that day we finally, through sincere effort and intention, pierce the Veil, and for a moment, gain direct access to it. We must always acknowledge and be grateful to It, for it is the Eternity in which our Cube of Light home is centered, our only separation from it is an invisible veil of light; and as with the cells of the Beehive, if removed, would become one whole hive, if the Veil were removed, we would all revert to the one whole Mind and lose our individuality – though not our Identity, just as the drops of water become one with the ocean only to express in other forms. "All of us one in the Father." Christ saw beyond the Veil – he knew the Whole and could stay centered in It.

In healing we oft times pierce this Veil and touch that Holy Mind and are healed. Prayer and the Silence help us to bypass the human mind, then one day we can retain contact for longer periods of time, until with just a thought – we are there. The block to contacting this Mind is being overly emotional, having rigid belief patterns or a busy mind filled with thoughts about much of our everyday chatter and problems. Focusing our mind is like getting a clear picture on a camera – we have to hold it <u>still</u> or we get a blurred picture. Getting through the <u>motion</u> of the body's five senses takes some time, but once you have tasted of the Inner Silence, you will be eager for more!

By threads of Light are we connected to this Father Mind as the facets in a diamond; and as Fibre Optics that carry messages throughout the physical world to everyone tuned in (via telephone, etc.), our prayers and efforts travel on these threads of light waves to our heavenly Father and impress our message upon Him and the distorted pattern is restored to wholeness and balance – we are healed! We have focused in and the Veil is rent. "Knock and it shall be opened unto you."

Disease, and problems as well, are distorted light wave patterns brought about at sometime during our journey through space, by our thoughts and emotions that were recorded on the body as memory patterns. Some are imposed from the outside, but <u>all</u> are a measure from which we should learn something. Each negativity that is corrected releases the energy held captive therein, and is used by the body for its healing, until without much effort our health improves, problems seem to resolve themselves, and our disposition is a delight with which to live.

Some problems that will not give in to prayer – may need a deeper therapy to get through the debris of the human mind, but regardless of the method used to clear the channel – it is always the Father Mind that does the healing. "I of myself can do nothing, the Father within, He doeth the works."

We can eliminate future build-ups of problems and keep our recording system in order, by reviewing, resolving, and making amends daily – the pay-as-you-go plan, instead of carrying the burden of unresolved debts that may later surface as problems or illnesses. By Grace are we healed, but there must be some effort on our part. The dessert of life comes only after many main courses are served.

And what is Grace? Webster describes it as the favor, the love that comes after our state of reconciliation to God.

"Not my will but Thine be done."

Grace is when the effort is no longer your own.

* * * *

73

A PRAYER

Father – my prayer each morning -
Noon -and night, is that I may love
And serve Thee, each moment with
Delight - -

As on wings of love my thoughts
Reach out to Thee- Take me with
You into Eternity - - -

Then - - soaring endlessly past time
And space, Eternal Love has brought
Us Face to Face.

* * * *

11
Our Body

Enfolded deep within the sheaths of this magical and mysterious body is hidden the All-Knowing and ever pure Spiritual Being which is you, held captive by the flesh until the day we perceive its importance in our life, then the search for Liberation begins. The greatest mystery of all waiting to be solved right within us, the mystery of our own spirituality, the Seed of which is certained to be in the lower left ventricle of the heart, the part of God within us.

It is interesting to note that in a film explaining the building of the embryo, it starts with the heart, the rest of the body being built around it – the place wherein the Word becomes flesh; the Word being your very own personal vibration and keynote, a gift from the Creator, expressing his Special Idea of you as a part of this many-patterned and oft time crazy, jigsaw like puzzle called Life, and the reason no two individuals are alike. Our fingerprints identify us while on earth – but the Word is our identification with God.

One way of finding your Keynote vibration is to play the tone that pleases you most on your piano, then make a harmonious cord of it, then play or hum it until you feel the vibrations throughout your entire body. If practiced, it can bring you into harmony with your Inner Self, just as a piano tuner harmonizes the tone of the piano to his Tuning Fork to bring it to a perfect pitch.

In Spiritual training we are taught that the heart is the home of the Spirit and to keep it pure. Then there is that ever mischievous Cupid who is always busy mesmerizing the Lovers of the world which sometimes brings a rude awakening; and - - that well known picture of Christ, "Knocking at the Door of the heart," with a Love that never changes; always – that secret place of Love, the Heart.

Before becoming visible, we are hidden within that Seed, just as the Oak tree is hidden in the acorn, waiting for that certain moment and those special Parents to whom we are drawn by the law of attraction, who will be the most suitable to help us work out our future in the world of time and space, and Lo! We're on stage. Our plan and purpose are packaged with us, the results in our life depending largely on how well we keep tuned into that Plan. Our parents give us our body but the responsibility for our life is ours, remember, we bring our own past with us, and we may be paying up or collecting the rewards this time, being careful, now that we're Aware, to record an even better reward at our next appearance.

Within the folds of this body are seven important Glands (the Jacob's Ladder of the Scriptures) known to us as: The Pineal and Pituitary in the head; the Thyroid at the throat, the Thymus in the chest, the Pancreas in the Solar

Plexus (abdomen), the Adrenals over the kidneys – and last, the Gonads in the pelvic area, in which lies the latent energy forces of the body. These glands are sometimes called the "motors of the body" as they have a hum and a vibration that can be heard and felt as we become more Aware. These "Invisible Guardians" (or glands) regulate our weight, growth, personality, and intelligence. Dr. Louis Berman details about this subject in his book called, <u>Glands</u> <u>Regulating</u> <u>Our</u> <u>Personality</u>. Upon the balanced functioning of these glands depends our good health. Emotional upsets and negative attitudes affect the chemical balance of our body, which in turn disturbs the rhythm of the glands, distorting our behavior pattern even to the point of killing ourselves or someone else. Our purpose in mentioning them here is to verify the important part they play, as a healthy body and mind is part of, and a necessity to, a happy life as well as to Transmutation, which means learning to direct our energy flow through refining our thoughts and emotions. Please note – that though you may not have emotional outbursts, does not always mean all is well, as the suppressed emotions (on hold or buried) work secretly in the deep subconscious of your mind causing abnormal behavior such as anger, overeating, poor judgment, or any action you did not decide to do consciously – it's the Reactive mind at work, compulsive behavior

Then there is the Brain, wired for sound by the electric threads of light to the Creators Mind, acts as a workshop, the <u>switchboard for His messages</u> to activate specific parts of the body via the nervous system, and lastly, the heart through which the Breath of Life is pumped to keep the entire organism alive and running; it's our vital connection with all of Life.

Now comes those shadow-like sheaths that interpenetrate our visible body, called the Mental or (casual), Astral, and Etheric bodies. These so-called bodies are energy fields and are enveloped within our physical body in a similar manner to those sets of Russian wooden dolls, which when opened, disclose a smaller and smaller doll within a doll; these bodies thus transmit the life force to our physical cell body.

First, we will describe the Causal or Mental body which has its beginning in the Great Father Mind – God, the Cause behind all that is. After It leaves its home there as one with the Whole (is projected by God's thinking) it separates, and a two-pole polarity is set up within our brain, the positive and negative, male and female, the pair of opposites.

This is where our free will and choice begins; what we do here is the cause of all happenings in our life. This Causal or Mental body is built by our thoughts, choices, and decisions, so when a problem occurs, ask first, "What am I doing or have done to cause this problem?" The next step is to Communicate with the other party and correct it as soon as possible, as any similar problem is compounded over the original, to continue the creation of the Reactive mind. This is how we keep our lifeline free of problems that become sub-conscious hang-ups. If not handled <u>now</u>, can become an illness later, as they simmer away within us.

In my First Grade Class, when the children came to me with a problem, I had them sit in a corner of the room and discuss it and then come to me with the answer. It was humorous to peek at them as they pointed fingers, scowled, even pushed, sometimes it ended with a handshake, but it always ended with – "It's O.K. now teacher." I never did find out what the problems were, but they were learning to solve them on the spot, themselves. It was such a happy classroom!

Now with adults it may take more patience, but communication and not getting even, is the answer or it may bring dire results. For remember, as soon as a motion is set up, what we choose to do will be to our sorrow or joy, and it can sometimes cause an endless chain of events, due to the rhythm of the "Law of Three." Dr. Russell calls this law the Voidance Principle. * (see end of chapter) The thought, the action, and the reaction of results.

Sometimes lack of healing is due to holding resentful thoughts about past grievances, forgiveness is the answer; and even though a person has transited to another dimension, asking forgiveness still works, as thoughts can penetrate <u>all</u>

dimensions and even reaches to the Sun in matters of seconds, Dr. Russell says.

Second, is the Astral body we will be discussing. Its function is to step down the powerful current of energy from the God Center, the main power field. It insulates and regulates the flow of energy according to our ability to balance and absorb it, and protects our body just as our homes are protected from too powerful an electric current, by transformer stations before our homes are connected to it.

In this Astral area we deal with our feelings and emotions, and be assured that the heat of the emotions causes "body quakes" that affect our body just as surely as an earthquake affects the earth. It may take days – even weeks to calm our feelings, which disconnects us from the Spirit until our equilibrium is restored. This body of feelings also generates and sparks the desire within our Soul to fulfill its dreams, as it impels us to action!

Third, the Etheric body. It is our Spiritual Counterpart, and absorbs and conducts the muted energy from the Astral body, activates and puts life into the atoms to start them spinning, and acts as a cohesive bond for the Astral and physical bodies between which it is sandwiched. It can be shattered by shock or stress, and requires some time reassembling itself just as a disturbed pool of water takes time to settle. It is in this Etheric body pattern that we feel as tho' the part amputated is still there, and still alive.

This trio of Spiritual bodies enveloped within the physical body forms a unified field through which the Spirit works. How to keep them in balance is explained in different ways throughout these pages. These bodies of atoms are all vibrating at a terrific rate of speed to generate the gravitational force that holds together our physical body to make us visible; and as Dr. Teller who Fathered the Atomic Bomb once stated, "If you could harness the electrons that spin around the atoms in the molecules of your body, you could fuel a large Industrial Nation for more than a week." Is it any wonder that the people trembled with fear and wonder, and the earth quaked, as the highly Spiritualized Atoms of Christ's Body were released into space at the time of His death?

How do we activate this latent energy in our bodies? First, through the relaxed quietness of Prayer or Meditation, this allows the Inner flow of energy to permeate, renew, and restore to balance, our busy body. As for sparking the physical body's energy field, it takes the minerals from Mother Earth, as the Spiritual and Physical should always work together as one united Pair. Energy is all we ever deal with whether plant, planet, animal, or human, and regardless of which dimension we function in or on, as we always have a body and it is always energy that moves it, and we are that Energy!

Lastly, to protect us from the surrounding atmosphere, our entire body is encircled with an oval shaped electronic field known as the Aura. It protects the physical body in somewhat the same way as the placenta protects the Embryo during its inner journey. It sometimes extends as far out from the body as six feet, is measurable, can be photographed (Kirlian photography), and its vibration is felt by persons in close proximity to us. Its' lines of force droop or swirl upward, according to our vital energy flow. The colors that vibrate through it range from dark earthy browns and greens, to delicate rainbow-hued pastels to white, and vary according to our development and mood changes. Pure Transfigured White Light is the Ultimate color as we grow into refined levels of higher Consciousness, as Christ at His Transfiguration. Negative emotions show as muddied and blurred colors, while positive feelings create clear and lighter colors, which also change according to our moods and health.

This Aura accounts partly for the Magnetism of the personality, and as it also acts as a screen for our projected thoughts, a good Seer can tell you much about yourself from past experiences as well as present ones from the thought pictures registered upon it. The Seers and Prophets of the Scriptures saw into deeper levels then everyday psychics do, and there are many today who have that ability. It comes through sincere seeking after the Truth.

Besides colors and lines of force, our problems are registered thereon as dark knots scattered throughout the Aura that imprison our vital energy until they are solved – at which time they disappear, like ironing out a wrinkle, then the energy flows freely again.

An interesting incident about Auras was told by Edgar Cayce, of Sleeping Prophet fame, of how he decided not to enter an elevator in which were several other people, because, even though the lights were lit, it seemed dark to him. As he went about shopping on that floor, he heard that the elevator had plunged into the basement and all the people therein were killed. He then realized the people had no Auras, accounting for the seeming darkness of the elevator. His extended vision had warned him and he obeyed, which saved his life. He then realized that people who were ready to leave the earth had no Auras, and he later observed this episode in many other cases. This surely makes us more aware that we are pinpoints of Light in this grand scheme of life, and we must do our utmost to keep it shining!

If you could see into your body with your Inner Eye, you would behold millions of pinpoints of light, looking more glorious than Los Angeles on a clear night! We were woven into visibility by that Light and are momentarily recreated and renewed, and held in Balance by that Light – The Light of God's All Knowing Mind. Do keep tuned into It.

In the sixties, so called "Health Nuts" were the rage, so when the book Sanpaku came out, this person decided to try her first diet by going on the Ten Day Purification Brown Rice Diet. You could eat all the rice you want any time you were hungry. Well, after a few days it was so boring, I fudged and added cinnamon one day, vanilla and gloves another, until finally, to keep from breaking it, I added Seven Grain bread (allowable) for the last two days, with that more then ever elegant flavor of butter on it! Two weeks later at our group meeting, a Special gentleman who had this Inner Vision exclaimed, "What have you done to yourself – I can see nearly all the way through your body!"

Well, his inner vision proved the results of the Purification diet, plus the loss of ten pounds, to my surprise. I was happy to regain it again. During that period of time my energy increased, my thinking was clear as a bell, and I looked radiant. This proves that our body is a permeable object and can be changed and kept in near perfect health in spite of our surroundings – through proper diet. If taking certain foods out of diets heals one, then it must be true that those foods cause the disease. As I understand it, we do inherit a number of tendencies to family disease but diet usually overcomes it; instead of antibiotics – try rest, diet and sensible living before disease gets a foot hold in your body. One glance will tell you how well disciplined in their eating habits people are – not to mention the cry for Government help at other people's expense (taxes, insurance) to repair their irresponsibility – don't always blame the genes either. In most cases it's the hand to mouth action that's to blame; not the genes!

What does all of this have to with Transformation?

As man evolved in a series of Rebirths from unawareness of Self, to awareness of Self as a human, then to greater heights of Self as a Spiritual Being, we wonder what the next dimensions will unfold to us. We live in the third dimension, but are learning about the fourth through Science and E.S.P., but what about the fifth, sixth and seventh? St. Paul spoke of the Third Heaven, and the Saints tell of the Ecstasy in dimensions beyond that, the ants know naught of us in their dimension, and we are becoming more aware and used to hearing of unusual happenings in space as well as on earth. Things are not really what they seem to be.

The rings of Saturn were thought to be clouds, and later were proven to be ice and rocks encircling the planet, held in space by the whirling forces of gravity to make beautiful picture patterns in the Heavens. It's all out there just waiting to be discovered!

Inner space and outer space have a correspondence, levels layered like a book upon a book, this makes life a progressive never ending adventure of new beginnings and endings, that when lived to our highest resolve, will instinctively lead us to our true purpose on earth; and to who we are, in ever unfolding experiences to bring it about, as God does not make foolishness – man takes care of that.

As man has evolved, so have plants. While learning to garden, I discovered the Blue Flowering plants were the latest color addition to be added to earths' plant family, a fragile color that fades easily. A short time ago delicate peach and lilac Roses came into prominence. One wonders what new colors will next take their bow as we move forward in time.

At one time, also, the human eye could detect only black and white, and had to evolve to see colors. Could color blindness be part of sight mutations? Natives moving out of treed jungles have to adjust their sight to a new spatial dimension. All of the Universe and everything in it is being Transformed, moment by moment.

We are hearing much now about Toxins that collect in the body cells due to chemicals in water, sprays, and food. These are often thought to be the cause of illnesses and aging. Our best known Vitamins of A, C and E, are among the top recommended detoxifiers clearing the body of debris, keeping it from aging and in better health.

All of this knowledge adds up to Transmutation, a big word for responsible everyday living, our Goal as we move into the Future. Self-conquest is the answer to a better and happier state of Inner Peace and a Peaceful world.

*Voidance Principle: (Also called the <u>Law of Three)</u>

Every effect of motion is voided as it occurs, is recorded (in its inert gases) as it is voided, and repeated as it is recorded.

See pg. 96 – No. 54 example – from Dr. Russell's A NEW CONECPT OF THE UNIVERSE.

12
Our Mother Earth
Variations of a Theme

O Earth thou cradle of Infinity, borning place of Man's becoming Self." Betty Mc K. - - - -

In all your Majesty, still spinning in space billions of years after leaving your home in the Sun. Made from the same substance of which our bodies are made; thought, light, energy, atoms, and gases; in need of heat and water to survive, and shaped into a sphere by the constantly whirling forces of gravity until space had been squeezed from between your atoms to just the right degree, to solidify this holy ground upon which your human family would tread; then to be seeded with the Living gases and atoms from our Father Sun, to bring forth His Creation – in pairs of opposites, Male and Female, so there could be the Joy of Loving to balance the hard work required of them during this grade of their Earthly journey thru endless space.

The earth too, has been transformed to keep pace with its human family through their different stages of growth and change. There is a comparison between the earth and human bodies. Its inner parts are marbled throughout with veins of ores, precious metals of gold, silver, and minerals, hollows of caves, pools of water, hard and soft areas, as our bodies also have.

On the surface of earth in place of hair, there are trees, grasses, and weeds of many varieties, so that when an area is scarred by flood, volcanic ash, or fire, mother earth immediately starts responding by giving birth to friendly new growth to heal its scarred surface, just as new skin recovers the damaged areas of our body.

Earth's core is composed of intense liquid heat, our body's blood temperature is 98.6, as heat is needed for life, as well as creating the pressures needed to Transmute bodies from one state to another. The earth's surface is burrowed into by billions of bugs, insects, and worms, to keep the soil workable and fertile, and provides the added bacteria necessary to enliven it. Our intestines are housed with friendly bacteria to help digest our food and keep the immune system healthy. Our bodies are about 80% water, while the earth's surface is covered with about 75% water. It's when the foreign bacteria overcomes the healthy ones that an illness sets in, so it is when earth's vascular system is overcome with poisons – it loses its ability to replenish itself. Drugs of all types kill good bacteria in humans while unwise use of poisonous chemicals and sprays damage the earth – and unbalance is at hand.

Right now our earth is struggling to regain its balance that has gone too far to the left, as has the balance in our Political System, and with Businesses and its workers. When greed for profit lets business disregard its workers, we are in deep trouble, which we are now witnessing; and when workers take advantage of their privileges by not giving full attention to their work, wasting time, taking extra unneeded days off, and filching property, are helping to destroy the company they work for, as well as themselves, as we also see now.

Everyone that works well, deserves a fair share of the profit as well as the Stockholders, and everyone that learns to spend well, will not be shackled with unnecessary debt. Balance is the word – plus patience.

What happens because of these changes? Those left to carry the burden, of the sell-out or cut back, are led into slavery – yes a different kind of slavery than those lashed on the back if the boat wasn't being rowed fast enough, or the slave too tired to carry on; it's slavery in that the one person carries the burden of the three or four who were dismissed – and the word for it today is Stress – one of our newest diseases, and we're left with the somewhat comforting thought that – at least we have a job. But what of the others? There is a hopeful sign that some Businessmen have read the symptoms and are doing their best to cooperate by inviting their employees to become a responsible part of the Company, a cooperative idea that brings more peace of mind and good will. It fosters a willingness on the part of the Workers to do better work, as they are now a part of the Plan – after all – what can one do without the other? They are one of the pairs of opposites, that will eventually have to come into a better balance or invite a greater disaster then we are now seeing. These far-sighted men are a blessing – we hope others will follow their example. It is not Government and business first – it is business and workers with Government invited when needed that matters.

The comparison doesn't stop there. The Van Allen Belt, the earth's Aura, and atmosphere science tells us, reaches up to twelve miles out from the earth to protect us from over bombardment of the Sun's cosmic rays. There is concern at this time about the rents appearing in the Belt, due to explosions of Atom Bombs, flouro-carbons, (then the worst of all Chernobyl). They cause the earth's temperature to rise, thus speeding up the melting of Ice Caps, which in turn raises the ocean's water level up to nine inches in one year and at one time, to seep into the fresh water wells of San Diego, California. An earlier period report during the late 50's revealed that there were 36,000 tons of Atomic debris in the atmosphere, encircling our earth, to be rained down on the food grown, then ingested by our cattle whose milk we drink, and whose meat we eat. Buried in the earth in their natural state these elements are harmless – it's when they are compacted into a form that they become dangerous, as Radiation speeds up the natural destruction to too high an intensity, and both humans and earth suffer the results, as it also causes the mutation of the genes' patterns. Who knows how many of today's illnesses are the results of this destruction?

Balance is said to be at a 90 degree angle and the speeding up of those intensities creates a disturbance in the orderly nature of things and we have the unbalanced wobbling effect, as our earth and its family is now said to be wobbling in space.

Deforestation of old trees is another problem as it unbalances the Carbon content of earth, which is the basis for all organic life; and with the erasing of the Amazon Rain Forest which supplies at least half of the worlds oxygen -our very breath is at stake! With the ocean's oxygen supply being poisoned, dead seas means dead inhabitants.

All of these mutations due to radiation are taking place momentarily – bit by bit and what to do about it should be our concern – or is your attitude – I won't be here – why should I care? Keeping in good health helps to combat some negative aspects of these changes; it's because all of Creation is an interlocking network, made of the same materials that we are affected in similar ways.

Another aspect of change for earth and its family is – that both started from a single position in time and space, and each has continually expanded, and or multiplied from one condition to another; at present the family seems to be "lost."

The breaking up of one solid land mass at the North Pole aeons ago, then gradually separating into what we now know as the Seven Main Continents, positioned at certain areas of our globe, with many varieties of change through periods of time. What a perfect balancing act that must have been for Mother Nature through whom the Creator works! I've wondered often, how the position of the earth changed to accommodate the distribution of these huge landmasses.

As Humanity multiplied to first live in groups, tribes, then families, and now many individuals prefer living alone. History records that King Tut originated the idea of families living together as they do today, because he dearly loved his sweetheart, and wanted her with him at all times, as men still lived separately in those days. Is today's problem with families staying together due partly to those past <u>instinctive</u> memories or integration? The urge of the Spirit is ever to return to the Oneness from which it came, while the urge of the flesh is to be recognized as an individual – in the blending of these two aspects – we see the struggle.

When our family moved from the Eastern U.S. to California, the first changes I noticed, besides the weather, were the beauty of the vegetables, but they lacked the delicious flavor of those of the East – due to not allowing the ground to rest during the Winter, I learned later; and secondly, the men of the East stayed with the group at parties or Family gatherings, while in California, the men separated, and gathered to talk man-talk while the women were left to talk about – you guess what.

Some of our older European Cultures still include the entire clan of relatives as part of the family unit – even to living together after marriage and children, and caring for their aged as well. Today, the Government has taken on more of these responsibilities, at the Taxpayers expense. What part does this play in the integrating of the whole?

Then there are families who separate, never to see each other again. As time goes on, the Individual has become more important than the Group. Nature seems to have as its intent, the Individuation of its human family, as well as the world – raising single Units, almost complete in themselves, our Leaders and Hero's, who should be examples of what every other one can become, if that is their intent. Life is always a choice. To what end will this individuation go? At this point it seems to have regressed, but the pendulum is still swinging.

The positive aspect of this change is the Quest for – Who am I – and what is my place in life? Learning to live from our own Creative Center, to fulfill our own dreams, instead of our life being determined completely by what family or religion we were born into, then being captured into that form, is oft times stagnation. One has to find for one's own sake, the answers to those questions. Experience is the teacher through which we find our own answers – advice can make us more aware, but it's the actions that record the results and bring about change.

To wrest your individuality from the mass or group – to find your own Life's Plan, and yet be in harmony and accord with all the rest, is not a simple task. It takes courage to break old beliefs and habit patterns, yet some World Leaders, some being ahead of their time, have done just that. Change promotes fresh new ideas – but if they are not centered – it can prove disrupting to Society.

Could a rare diamond be seen as a priceless gem among hundreds of others, until it was placed in its own special setting? Could a planet become a beautiful and useful home if not separated from its mass of "Star Stuff?"

Follow your own dream, upset the applecart – break old habit patterns, but do it as honorably, and as painlessly as you can for honest Commitments should never be broken without the consent of all parties concerned, as that is a necessary part of good Character and our own integrity. Our Birthright is our God given choice, and remember – Nature is ever at a constant to keep change alive and moving forward and up, within the Law, and if humans will allow it – with Joy! This is true Transmutation and Individuation.

To be really free in your Soul – you must have some sort of a Spiritual conviction, as there is only One Creator, and many aspects of belief in Him; and when you sincerely do your best with those beliefs – like Saul on his way to Damascus, who was changed in the twinkling of an eye from a rebel against Truth to an ardent promoter of It, you will be <u>led</u> to your right destination. Are you willing to give it a try?

As we've explored some of the facts about Creation, we've found that the pairs of opposites prevail in all things; hot and cold, male and female, the lock and its key, etc. and the reason is – that there must be at least two, for anything to inter-change, the cause of all motion.

Another thought provoking question, have you noticed the Earths opposites? Belting the Equator, we see the Tropic of Capricorn on the South portion, and the Tropic of Cancer on the North position. Astrologically, they are the Father and Mother Principles, respectively, while on the Calendar they stand six months apart – the opposites.

Calling the Observatory, I found they were named that because they were nearest to these two Constellations at the equator. The Dictionary states that each of these two circles on the Celestial sphere limit the Sun's apparent annual path, and either of the two corresponding parallels of latitude, including the Torrid Zone, the Region between them. All things are limited by Universal Law to keep them in order.

One wonders what the early Map Makers had in mind as they named all of those Sky Symbols – why and how those Ideas were formulated. It would take research into Ancient Astronomy, to uncover the reason, I was told.

Then too, from the heart of our earth's equator originates the winds and clouds that carry the life giving moisture that blankets the earth to refresh it after a depressing heat wave, the winds that carry the Winging birds, on their air pockets, to and fro from their nesting grounds, to other parts of the world at the change of Seasons. Then there are the powerful winds that carry seeds from one continent to another to continue its species, and perhaps to cross breed to start new ones; winds from North, South, East and West, unseen, but accounted for by our Scientists, and sometimes by the destruction they leave behind, but ever reminding us that we are carefully being watched over by the "Great Cosmic Eye," that keeps all things in balance, tho' it seems sometime to the contrary – to build – rebuild and renew all of Earth's terrain.

The wind currents and ocean's water currents, distributing their gifts as they pass our way, all for the use and protection of the earth's Family of Creatures ever obeying the rhythms of the Infinite. Did you know that on our Northern Hemisphere the water goes down the drain clockwise, while on the Southern Hemisphere it turns counter-clockwise? The pair of opposites again.

Then too, human nature is also both male and female, in one person. The female lies latent in the male, and within the female is the submerged male. If either was a pure strain, they would be either a hard, aggressive and cold hearted male, or a too soft, permissive, overly emotional female. As we experience life, we learn to blend these two sides of ourselves to become a balanced individual. A book written by John Sanford, about <u>The Invisible Partners</u>, describes the needs of, identifies and explains, in an interesting manner, how this pair within us functions, helping us to understand others as well as ourselves.

In marriage we are learning to balance two opposite personalities, and if we understand what we are trying to accomplish, the task can become more like a game, instead of a struggle, as we communicate our needs to each other. Then of course there's the children with their opposites. It goes on and on, the entire world and its pairs of opposites, interchanging and growing until each one reaches their own balanced zenith. This growth can be a very harmonious affair, as resistance to our problems prolongs their solutions. Learn to yield.

On this journey through earth life, evolution comes with the transmutation of the cosmic cell and Consciousness until it reaches near perfection; and as with our body, the earth also is a network of pulsating, invisible, electric threads of Light through which the Creator transmits His ideas and feelings, and directs all changes in the evolutionary life processes of growth.

Life is the Light of God's loving thoughts in action, permeating the density of earth as well as our bodies.

This Weaver of Light who has threaded us in our jeweled cocoons, into the Cosmic Web of Destiny, our bodies – the strings of Life upon which he strums his Cosmic Melodies.

There comes a time when the perfecting process within has been accomplished, our desires have been fulfilled, and our visits to earth are completed. We are then ready to move on to higher levels of Consciousness – else what is the purpose? Was it all worth it? The Promise of Eternal Life and Peace makes it so.

And with an Ode of Joy in our hearts, we say - -

"O MAKE HASTE!"

* * * *

The Light Of Love

As the sunflower, whose tightly compacted seeds are enfolded within the Heart of its protective petals until ripe enough to be scattered to earth to Multiply its gifts- - -so are we held within the protective Light of Gods Throbbing heartbeats of Love until we become points of Light that radiate His Divine Love to others in the world.

So spreads the gift of Love – for Love is the ultimate goal of Life. Love Is the Light of God in action – for this is Holy Ground.

* * * *

13
Soul and Spirit
The True Self

Breathed outward from a still point beyond time and space wherein the heart of God is hidden, the Spirit of Life moves forth to touch the hearts and souls of its creation, as well as all of Nature, with the magical urge to bring forth its new Life - - and Spring stirs within the bounteous bosom of Mother Earth.

In the deep brooding stillness of winter, when the unseen mystery of Regeneration is birthing, hidden from mortal eyes, the rest from action builds this new energy to its peak; and at that certain time during the middle of the month of February each year, the pressure generated in the root systems of trees and plants awakens, causing the sap in the trunks of the trees to surge upward spilling into their branches, and swelling the pod-like coverings of the buds to the bursting point, allowing the blossoms to escape to display their delicate fairy-like beauty, and to announce to the world that – Spring is here! And once again their pungent fragrance is wafted on the breath of the airwaves, maybe to touch the hearts of a pair of special Lovers, who respond to the call, and spring is born. And once again, Nature clothes itself with a fresh Aura of greenery that shimmers with its new life as it eagerly reaches out to imprint itself on the hazy, grayed, skyline of space; and once again, God views his Earthly Kingdom with the satisfaction of a Maestro after the applause of a successfully orchestrated symphony – and the Dance of Spring is on! The Transfiguration of Nature has once more been accomplished.

Within the hearts of the human family, the call to mating also dons a fresh new look and romance stirs within with renewed vigor. The birds and bees adding their love chirps, and drones of "Homage to the Great High King" – as if to give proof that – even tho' everything's been done before – it's all new once again, and that Rebirth is a Joyous affair!!

The Easter parade bursts forth its sense of beauty with outrageously decorated hats, towering perilously high on the brows of Elegant Ladies with strangely imaginative trimmings that far out does "a nest of robins in her hair," while the fresh delicate colors of Spring apparel, heralds the expectation of the exciting summer months ahead.

But there's more to Easter than meets the eye; what goes on inside of you is really what Easter is all about. Take for example, the forty day period before Easter Sunday when the age-old custom of abstaining from negative habits, thought, word, or otherwise; in order to prepare and purify oneself, to give special meaning to that most glorious celebration of the year, the Resurrection – the Promise that Life is Eternal, and Christ being the only human ever recorded to have accomplished that feat – would change, forever, the way the world would understand the purpose for which we were born, for our very own body is the Birth place of this transfiguration.

Before the beginning of time, during the embryonic stage of creation – there was only one complete Soul, centered by the Light Divine, the Spirit, and the Desire of the All-Knowing Mind to bring forth this Panorama of Creation. When it was decided to project this Idea into a form – the One Soul was divided into many individual Souls (as in the Beehive) then the Word was Spoken – and we each received our Name – the Keynote Vibration that distinguished us one from the other – and our Atomic pattern was recorded forever in the Ethers, the Book of Life – as has been told of in the Greatest of Stories. Now, this Soul is composed of Life, Love, and Feeling, and is our personal lifeline through which the still small Voice of the Holy Spirit ever whispers to us our purpose, and keeps us centered: it's the Genii that brings forth our desires. And when you are Truly inspired, or in the silence, reveals Itself in many wondrous ways: as everything worth having requires an effort, we must woo the Soul to become a functioning point in our lives. "Incite the Muse," is the way Brahms spoke of It as he composed his famous music, and became angry if disturbed – lest the Message that prevailed would escape him.

The Soul contains all of our unfulfilled desires from the past as well as the present that we came to earth to fulfill – plus the memory of what not to do, which acts as our Conscience, all based on the <u>Law</u> <u>Of Balance</u> – a learning process. This also is where man's dilemma comes in; freedom of choice if not based on the Inner Wisdom, may lead us through a maze of mistakes that we could mostly have avoided.

Now, if you should dream of being lost, can't make connections when traveling, or can't find your way home, it's your Soul warning you to get back on the right track – you've detoured – learn to make better decisions.

Dreams can be a helpful part of making wise decisions in our life, as they are personal Messages from the Holy Spirit who is ever our Guide. They range from warnings, to predictions of things to come, and tell us of our inner growth; and as we move up the Jacob's Ladder – they change from black and white scenes to beautiful colored ones, telling us of our successes and where we need to change.

The Bible notes many instances of dreams forewarning the people to prepare for a change in times, such as the Pharaoh's dream of the Seven lean and Seven fat ears of corn, for which Joseph was called to interpret its meaning to him. It warned of their coming famine, so the people could prepare for it.

Dreams still hold their place in today's world, as man and God will always speak to each other in the

Silence.   Sleep closes off the body's sensing motion, and the message gets through.   To understand dreams is wisdom in itself.

The steps that we take while moving up this Jacob's Ladder of Consciousness, rooted in Eternity, are where we wrestle with the right and wrong of the physical senses, the way in which we develop the added Awareness of seeing, hearing, and sense of smell; as we reach out with our sensing, our inner knowing extends itself to us and when they meet, the ladder has served its purpose. We have crossed the line of separation and are now centered in our Knowing, which is the part of God within us.   With practice, it will bloom into full Cosmic Consciousness, our Liberation!

The development of this Knowingness starts as hunches, feelings, then peaks at Knowing, and when you know you know, nothing can deter you from your course. From then on life becomes a joy – for the individual Soul has touched its Source – its Oneness with the Whole. In your Soul you are free. Everyone is equal in Spirit – it's while on earth that there are inequalities; thus our degree of effort to improve, determines our level of existence "By your works shall you be known."

Our body is the flower of our Soul's desires, much as the lily is the result of its stages of growth through the muddy soil as it reaches out to the light, to tower on its slender swaying stem in all of its trumpeting purity and gracefulness. Christmas gave us the Babe, and Easter gives us the Transfigured man. The Journey has been completed and clearly defined by the examples of Christ. The Soul's atoms live on Light and Love while the senses live mostly on things – until we reach out for higher ground. As we become more aware that all Souls are part of the same Soul, which is Gods Soul, the mirage of humanity takes on a new look. Love displaces the distortions that separate us – for a problem is but love – waiting to be released from its bindings.

We take many steps up many small mountains, 'til finally we ascend the greatest one, where we know our Oneness with our Creator and the Whole – this is when, it is said by the great Prophets, that there is no more returning to earth. We move into higher levels of learning. Brothers we are all one; this was Beethoven's vision.

Creation is made up of many levels of vibrations, from the coarsest to the finest, of which the Ladder is a Symbol of the Way. As we go through these liberating transformations, we learn what it means to bring forth the Gifts of the Spirit, don the wedding garment, keep our light shining, and to make right decisions. Suddenly everything seems to line up unexpectedly; your refinement attracts this to you. And as you count your Blessings, your heart is filled with a new kind of love, and you join happily in sharing these blessings with others.

This is the much talked of Divine Romance of the Soul, the Inner marriage, for which everyone is instinctively seeking, and of which the human marriage is a symbol. Often times when this Inner Unity has been made, one finds their true physical mate, the search for which is a whole "nother" story.

* * * *

What was happening in those earlier days <u>before</u> Easter became known as a Sacred Feast? Christ's three short years of public life held the events that the Apostles would record, and this is how it unfolded itself to me:

There was Talk of a Strange Man who walked through the village Streets, and claimed, when asked who he was, "When you have seen me you have seen the Father, for I and my Father are One." "What manner of speaking is this?" the crowds asked of each other, and just by spitting on mud and plastering it over their eyes – the blind were healed and could see! Walking among the lame, crippled, and all sorts of sinners, who responded to His gentleness and kind words, were delivered from their sick-beds and rose up to shout praises of his works! Those hobbling on crutches, dropping them, threw up their hands in surprise, to walk again – shouting words of gratitude for their new freedom.

Crowds of hundreds collected to follow this Amazing Man - - the healed, the curious, the forgotten, the sinners, and those still in the middle of the road – the doubters – all were eager to hear his fresh new words of hope, or to judge Him. His love was the Magnet that drew them, and he filled their hungry hearts with new Life when he said, "Thy sins are forgiven thee – go and sin no more."

The freedom of forgiveness lifted them out of their bondage of retribution and gave new life to their sick bodies, minds, and Souls. Jesus did not require they ask for forgiveness – he gave it freely, as with his Inner Knowing he could see their hurts and needs, and extended his healing love to them. Their belief in his words was the cure. "According to thy belief shall it be done unto you."

He drove the Money Changers from Houses of Worship, and confounded the crowds when he commanded the elements to obey him – and they did! This caused some doubters to say he did it by the power of the devil – while to others whose hearts were touched by his words, it brought fresh inspiration into their hopeless lives, as those were days of high taxes, and much cruelty and oppression by the Rulers – but at last – here was a new hope!

They, not knowing of his yet to be fulfilled Mission, escaped the knowledge of his personal heartache as he wept in the Garden, and prayed that he might be released from the great responsibility he was about to encounter. But when he was sure it was part of his Destiny, he acquiesced with –

"Father, not my will but Thine be done." He never complained.

The Crucifixion and Resurrection were the result of his efforts to help others and to bring the new message of – "Love ye one another as I have loved You," into the world. It was so unbelievable, that he later invited Thomas, his Disciple who doubted he was the Risen Christ, to place his finger inside the scar of the wound on his side as proof of his Resurrection, which brought forth from Jesus, the oft heard phrase-"Blessed are those who have not seen and believed."

Then it was Jesus time to go to Jerusalem, and as he came into that town, the crowds who had witnessed his Miracles, ran before him and stripped palm fronds from the trees and placed them on the pathway to honor his coming. As he rode, silently, over them on the back of his donkey, they shouted, "Blessed is the King of Israel that cometh in the Name of the Lord." This is now celebrated as our Palm Sunday, the week before Easter.

This was to be the final phase of his three years of Service to the Seekers; here he would gather with his Disciples, whom he had chosen from among his earliest Followers, (as he knew their hearts were ready to give all), for the Last Supper, the Betrayal by Judas, and finally that painful walk to Calvary the Mount of Skulls, (as crucifixion was a common punishment in those evil days); the place where he would give proof to the world of Life over Death.

This ended some of the most important events of the Period before the Resurrection in those earlier times, now celebrated by most Churches as our Lent and Easter Sunday.

While the meaning of the Crucifixion is crucial in our development, it is the Triumphant Resurrection that is the purpose of it all. What is the meaning of the Crucifixion in our lives today? It is moving out of our fixed negative ideas and habit patterns, and the Resurrection is our effort at practicing the Holy Presence momentarily, to become the master of our lives in unison with our Creator, as did Jesus.

* * * *

During the forty days after the Resurrection, the Apostles must have been filled with wonder and questions as they gathered together to review the strange events that had transpired over the many past months.

The Transfiguration on the Mountain Top with Peter, James, and John, who witnessed how Jesus stood before them, and His garments were as white as the Light, and a Voice from a heavenly cloud saying-"This is my Beloved Son in whom I am well pleased, - "Here Ye Him!"

Then there were the Miracles of walking on the water, the multiplying of the loaves and fishes, and

– the astonishment of raising Lazarus from the dead – even after three days. And now, even more mysterious, was the Resurrection – the empty Tomb!

They must have felt the sadness that they might never see their Lord again, as they did not as yet know of the sayings of the Scriptures. Christ had revealed many of his secret abilities as proof of this Inner Power, to inspire them to carry the Message of what the future new Age of Man held – where good <u>would</u> prevail. Hadn't he said, "I have many things to tell you, but you cannot understand them now," and "Greater works than I do, you shall do," even, "I shall see you again, and your hearts shall rejoice!" Then why did he leave us, and where did he go? It seemed as tho' he had forsaken them.

Then it happened – during one of their many gatherings, from out of nowhere, Jesus appeared and stood in their very midst!! Can you imagine their surprise, and how they must have eagerly questioned and clung to him, fearing he might leave them again?

After he had hushed their excitement, he spoke to them of things to come, to prepare them for their Mission, also to warn them of the trials, ridicule, and rejection, even unto death, as they carried this message of Repentance and Salvation, the steps to Transformation for the New Dispensation – as spoken of in the New Testament. It was a drastic change of ideas, when compared with the Old

Testament, of an "eye for an eye," the get-even method. Instead, Jesus said – "Do good to those who hate you, forgive a thousand times over, lest what you do unto others return unto you doubled," – our mirrors of light!

As you read through the Old Testament of an eye for an eye, and a tooth for a tooth, you can see why those ideas would be highly resisted in their discriminating Society. The fact that Jesus worked Miracles, hob-knobbed with sinners, and suggested casting the mote form their own eye first, broke agreement with their manmade laws; His idea being, to gain control over one's own self and lower nature, which in today's world of profligate living and unbelief, also needs much change.

As the days went on and other meetings had taken place, with many friendly chats with their master, again, came the call to go to Jerusalem. Questions probably raced through their minds as to what would happen next – would they see him – and what more would he share with them?

And it came to pass that it was the day of the Ascension, that unexpected event that would take their Beloved Lord's person from them for good.

In silence they waited – <u>again</u> Jesus appeared in their midst – and as they questioned him persistently about his promises, he comforted them with the words, "I will be with you always. Even unto the end of time, but if I go not, the Comforter cannot come." Their pleadings burdened his heart, and he reassured them of his love for them saying tenderly – "I go to prepare a place for you, so that where I am, you may also be.".... "Love ye one another, my peace I give unto you." As he finished speaking those words, and while they yet gazed upon him with such love, a soft cloud of Light encircled his body, and as their wondering eyes followed it as it lifted him toward the heavens – he disappeared from their view.

The pain of the final parting with their Beloved Lord at this last meeting, was more than they could bear, and the lamenting went on and on, until Peter, who was left in charge, reminded them – that the Scriptures had foretold of all of these things.

Several days later, again a message came to meet in the Upper Room in Jerusalem and wait--- and it states there were one hundred and twenty of his closest Followers present. It was to be the day we would call Pentecost.

Their anticipation was at its <u>peak</u> as they waited – for what? When suddenly a rushing wind swept throughout the room, and before their astonished eyes, Tongues of the Holy Fire rested on the heads of each one present and their bodies shook as the power of the Spirit thrilled within them, and they heard themselves speaking in many tongues, each understanding it in his own language. They had been opened up to Cosmic Consciousness; now they understood with a new Inner meaning the Parables that never were quite clear to them. This time they knew their purpose and it was revealed to them, also, who they were, and they accepted their Mission to preach the Gospel, and received the power to work Miracles and heal, as Jesus had done, to preserve and carry these Truths to the future generations – their Gift to us.

A peace now settled upon them: At last they knew their Jesus had kept his promise to send the Holy Spirit to them and they went forth to spread the Gospel to all who would listen and accept it, and it is said – many Miracles were performed in his Name, and to all who accepted was given the power to become Sons of God.

The energy infusion of the Holy Spirit, literally transforms the Atomic structure of your body and moves you out of the vibration of your old habit patterns into a higher level of functioning; just as a space shuttle is propelled into space by a series of transforming energy units, in sequences, then drops the used shell, to use its next quantum of energy units to project it higher into space, until it reaches its goal.

Thus are all things Transformed by this Holy Power, called by different names when used for different purposes, but all power is always extended from "The One," through the many.

From then on 'till this very day the Word goes forth to all who choose to align themselves with its positive power. It holds its own despite all efforts to extinguish it, and will do so until <u>all</u> have heard the Story, "If I be lifted up – I will bring all others unto Me." This is also our purpose.

* * * *

It took many decades of terror before much change was noticeable; then came the Roman Empire, its Gladiators, and Christians who were thrown to the lions to be eaten alive, as entertainment for a blood-thirsty mob of ruling spectators, who revelled in its cruelty.

Then there were the Crusades in the name of Religion, when anyone's belief in God warned them to hide in the Catacombs to survive. Each step forward had its backward flow.

At the closing of this period of time, at the meeting of the Nicene Council, it was decided to expunge from the Books of the Bible, the Verses that carried the idea of Reincarnation, as they felt people would not change as quickly, believing they had more than one chance; the idea of a truly just God – for remember – free choice was <u>man's</u> misuse of good.

So here we have the control element put into place. The Hierarchy then was set up and branched into many different types of control other than the Old Testament, never-the-less control. The Church of Rome became the all-powerful Ruler and with some trickery behind closed doors, that evil element that often times creeps into the best of institutions, overpowered the efforts of the truly dedicated ones. The rebels then set out to pillage the churches and gather into their power, all they could control, some of the events at which we are told Martin Luther rebelled, and was excommunicated from the Catholic Church. This period became known as the Reformation, and it was the beginning of the many denominations of religion, as we know it today. Pope Paul II has most humbly and graciously apologized for all of those former wrong doings – too late? Yes – but acceptable.

And so we arrive at today's world, still at war, one Nation against the other, not only for Religious reasons, but for their natural resources as well. We still have repression of religious belief – note the constant effort to erase all traces of our Historic Religious Symbols from public view and use, which has allowed disrespect for a Creator, and the lawlessness of freedom without restraint. Then there's the extermination of millions of humans by bombs, and nerve gases that leave men half alive. Will humans ever come to their senses, or has earth come to be just a body parts arena? This is evolution at its worst.

A Messenger came to save the world at one time – who or what will happen to save it this time? And what will Archeologists who exhume our Civilization's History find? Will false arms, legs, and plastic joints and mutilated bodies, from embryos to the eldest, bear witness of our undisciplined culture?

In today's world of uncertainty and pressures, many people are turning their thoughts once more, to this Inner world of comfort, and the many Religious movements tell us that the Search is alive and moving forward; the Holy Spirit is once again being felt. Its plan and purpose has been with us since we were first conceived in the Mind of the Creator, the truth of who we are has ever been with us – it just got covered up with miles and miles of memories of the lessons we were learning until – we make that Decision – then we, too, can receive the gift of the Holy Spirit and learn the Inner Secrets as did the Disciples. Thus we come to know that everlasting Peace and Love, and we are never alone again; then we become cosmically aware that we are all Sons of God who came from the farthest Star in the heavens, to inhabit a body made visible, through which we could again return in full Wisdom and understanding to our original home – as was also foretold in the Scriptures, "For were we not made higher than the Angels," says the Psalmist.

This beautiful story of the Spirits descent into matter to teach mankind how to overcome the world and the idea of death is celebrated from Christmas to Easter.

We now need no confessor or mediator, because the only separation between us and our Creator is a silken Veil of Light – so fragile that the slightest whisper or pure thought penetrates to His ever loving ear, and so strong that only the pure in heart can pierce it. All of this comes to us through the Lessons of Christ – who reminded his Disciple John, of what the Psalmist said: "Know ye not that ye are gods?" shall we add – in the process of re-awakening?

Our Country's gangs of all types are looking for a way out – be it right or wrong – of the unbalanced conditions that the un-regenerated part of man has created by his lust for power, greed, and lack of sharing – the cause of the world's undoing. But man will pay and pay – until he <u>knows</u> that love is the lesson he must learn, and that there <u>is</u> a Greater Will than his; and whatever pain it takes to realize this fact – even to a cataclysm – will prevail, until we learn that – <u>God</u> <u>always</u> <u>has</u> <u>the</u> <u>last</u> <u>word.</u>

* * * *

<u>COMMUNION</u>

O divine One within me –
My heart beats with the rapture of Thy Love –

How precious are the moments I spend with Thee-

Thy gentle love enfolds me like softly feathered
Wings.

What love Thou hast for us mortals –
What patience in our struggle to find Thee.
What joyousness at our return!

Oh! That I may have the patience to love others –
Till they, too, may know Thee as Thou art.

* * * *

14
The Heavens Declare The Glory of The Lord
What If – and What Then?

Would it take you by surprise to hear that Astronomers are saying that the Orion Nebulae, about 1,500 light years from our earth in the spacious sky, is the borning place of Stars, where they are created, perhaps as homes for the future tenants of the Universe?

And even tho' it is six trillion miles away, nested in the arms of our Galaxy, it shines so brightly that it can be seen on a clear night in the Northern sky, with the naked eye?

And, if, I wondered, stars are born there do they carry the seed patterns for all of their future family of planets and inhabitants as the Sun does in our Galaxy? And if that's where Stars are born – who is behind their borning – what is the Cause of their beginnings?

And would it fill you with wonder, that there is a beginning place we call Heaven, from which the Great Spirit spoke the Word with such Power, that it caused the Universe to form and the earth to become the place where the Word could become flesh, so that He could dwell amongst us to experience Himself as Human?

And what if you were <u>sure</u> now, that the Doorway to Heaven was out there in the physical star filled time and space Arena, and that someday you <u>knew</u> just where you were going to be – what then?

And what if all of the out-of-the-body and near death experiences in which people tell of the beauty that is seen there, and you know for certain you would meet old friends when you arrived, even former enemies, about whom you held thoughts of unresolved resentment that could be seen because of the transparency of the mind – with no dense body to hide them – what then?

Then again, what if this <u>is</u> where the Creator and his realms of Angelic Hosts of which we hear are abiding and into which, someday, we would be welcomed; how would you feel about facing all the things you <u>knew</u> were wrong, then went ahead and did them anyhow? And suppose that all of the stories you heard about Heaven are true, and you do have to account to the last farthing for all the misdirected thoughts and deeds. And perhaps to experience the same thing you did to others? – What then?

Is this what you feel this lifetime has been all about – and maybe it seems true now, that the Spirit of you does return at another time, in another body

– for a chance to correct and balance these misdeeds-could that be part of your <u>present</u> dilemma and why things seem so difficult and unfair?

Is this where our Father who art in Heaven dwelleth – the place Jesus spoke of when he said: "I go to prepare a place for you." And if you knew for sure, all of this was not just your imaginings – what difference would it make in your life <u>today</u>?

How would you feel about the scoffing you did at the ridiculous idea that anywhere there could be a real Heaven – least of all that you might gaze at it in the Star-lit nighttime sky?

Some amazing things have come to pass – even ancient predictions – in our century, and speaking of the Last Days – is a murmur that has grown louder each year. Are you ready for this Fantastic Place? An old saying, that coming events cast their shadows – is this the Shadow?

And what if the Many Mansions Christ spoke of, are the Planets in Outer Space – the stepping stones from which other more transfigured Beings than our human family, can span the heavens as easily as the speed of light, or as easily as we send our rockets into space; or that some of the lesser developed ones, might be on their journey to experience life on our Planet to learn the Law of Balance as we did before moving on to higher levels of learning? Or, that some souls who are ahead of their time are among us today. What of that?

There were a few well-known Way Showers of whom you may have heard or met, who, because of their extended Vision and Awareness knew that they came from the Star called Sirius or Canis Major, situated below the belt of Orion in the Southern sky of our Galaxy. Does that make you wonder?

Is this where we put on the body incorruptible that St. Paul spoke of? Where we can pick it up or lay it down as Christ did? And if so - Then what?

Many of these questions have been answered to my satisfaction and is the main reason why Transformation is <u>so</u> important, for it is said, only the Pure in Heart shall see God.

Down through the Ages, the Myths and Folklore have included the Story in the Sky, as does the Bible Scriptures, and other Great Spiritual Books, as part of the Theme of Life. Did they, in their wise but rugged innocence, know of these Secrets because they lived closer to Nature then we do – were more child like?

Much gratitude should be directed to those forerunners whose Records are Guidelines for our decoding, when the time was ripe, and as we grew out of our blindness, came to see them to be true! How much time have we spent chasing the ghost of things, believing them to be real; and are we now ready to put first things first?

A world famous doctor of brain surgery – demonstrated on television with his anesthetized patient, how, by touching certain parts of the exposed brain with a surgical instrument, the patient would describe experiences that happened to her during this lifetime, as well as other periods of time; the surroundings, clothing, and incidents from former periods of history in which she knew herself to be the Experiencer, thus showing that the records of our many past lives as well as present, are filed and recorded in our memory patterns – else how the child Prodigy's, and De-Je-vous people experience? Is Science coming to prove that many lives are a normal part of the sequences of our Journey through the Universe? If so – what then?

Is it too late to start changing now? Never! Sometimes the late moment can be the most glorious of all, and as we finish our earthly journey, the Wisdom and Loving Qualities we have developed are all recorded and balanced in the Book of Life, and forever bring forth their Blessings into future expressions. And as we consider that we did the best we could at that moment – we can Be at Peace, for our Loving Father wants us all to come into the Fold; the Fold being that wonderful Peaceful State of Mind that comes with Spiritual Alignment, for again, are we not gods in the making?

So as Life closes its door on our allotted time, we are wiser for having experienced another chapter in the Drama of Creation – we who came forth from the heart of God, shall once more return to His Bosom – for out of Love were we born and unto Love we shall return, and as we come to <u>believe</u>, it is proven to us.

What then, O when, and O what Joy!!

* * * *

Some Afterthoughts

At the closing of these chapters came a European Journal Newsflash on television about the latest happenings in Russia.

It seems that thousands of people had developed healing abilities and were using them to heal each other. Displayed among a large crowd on the street was a table with different types of apparatus used to heal; pendulums, metal rods, crystals, and laying on of hands.

There had been much insistence by some, wanting the medical association to investigate this strange phenomena at which up until now, they had winked.

At last, responding to those demands, a group of people were chosen to be diagnosed. Standing before this lined-up group, was a rather plump, white haired middle-aged woman with her hand outstretched toward them and she diagnosed accurately, all of their internal organs, to the satisfaction of the Medical group, who were present to judge the healing.

The doctors had previously tested the thousand of others, and decided that there were five hundred who actually had the ability to heal. When asked how this came to be, the people claimed that it had all started with headaches after the explosion at Chernobyl; then the healing powers developed.

As we have observed, atomic energy is intensified light waves of radiation and the pressure of light causes things to transmute from one state to another. Here was a negative happening that also had brought a positive result. In this case, the woman had become clairvoyant – the ability to see into and through a solid mass, or object. I wondered – were they able to heal each other of the damage done to their bodies by the radiation? They did not specify this; maybe we will hear more about the results as time goes by.

It is interesting to note, that the people connected it with the Chernobyl incident, which seems to verify the results of transmutation. For as the energy response is released within our body, it moves upward through the Centers (the Chakras) through prayer, meditation, or otherwise, and we do have a reaction in our body, because it frees us of old habit patterns that have clumped within us, allowing new abilities to develop.

Some of the symptoms of release may be sneezing, rashes, colds, ringing in ears and perspiring, so if you are in good health otherwise this could be caused by these changing pressures. So flow with these changes, knowing it is some of your new growth sprouting.

And as the sublime, cohesive power called Love, that binds together the entire Universe, wends its way to the top of the head to find its resting place within you while yet on earth, the sleeping Lotus Blossom of Wisdom gently unfolds its petals to reveal in a most wondrous fashion, the Gifts of the Spirit, the inner Spiritual world, as well as its counterpart the earth, then life has fulfilled its basic purpose in you as an individual.

From then on a new zest for life seems to enter because of the greater understanding that results, and an inner happiness that allows us to accept the goodness of life despite appearances to the contrary. Perhaps a new talent you never dreamed you had will raise its wobbly head to be nurtured to fulfillment. And there's that feeling like a secret smile inside you that seems to attract all kinds of surprises into your life from everywhere, from now on!

It's still happening today as in the days of yore, the Gifts of the Holy Spirit; healing, prophecies, and miracles, inviting you to join in that greatest of Adventures, that Special moment, when we humbly come Face to Face with the Holy Spirit, and we give birth to the Self – the True Image in which we are created, as we yet float in this Sea of Life, the Spiritual amniotic Substance, called time and space.

It has happened to me – It could happen to you too.

Thus ends a Chapter of the "Stormy Cosmic Love Affair" of Mother Earth and her family of

Souls as, together, they wend their way into the Mist of Eternity.

* * * *

I PLUCKED A STRING

I plucked a string and you were born,
Of all Thy heavenly beauty shorn.

To search that finite land afar,
To learn to love where ere you are - -

A wanderer in the maze.

No soul can know that Peace Sublime
Anchored to the wheel of time-

Till he look inward, low Behold!
The sheep returneth to the fold.

Freed from all on earth he found-
To be mortal is to be dead!

Yes - I plucked the string that borned
You to the earth-but Thy yearning soul
Found not to quench it thirst – for -

"I Am" the fountain from which life springs
But the lure of the earth entrances Thy
Senses with the song she sings.

The time is come when thy Inner Sight
Is awake!

The dream is past-

Thou art returned to My bosom at Last!

BIBLIOGRAPHY

Manly Palmer Hall
Man The Grand Symbol of The Mysteries

Dr. Walter Russell
Secret of Light
A New Concept of The Universe

Lao and Dr. Walter Russell
Scientific Answer To Human Relations

Dr. Gustaf Stromberg
Soul of The Universe

Herman Aihara
Acid and Alkaline

John Sanford
Dreams: Our Invisible Guardians

Dr. Fritz Kunkel
Creation Continues

Radhakrishnan
Bhagavadgita

Swami Radha
The Divine Light Invocation

I

*** All Bible quotations are from the New
        Testament.

*** All poems are by the Author.

*** The Author is aware that some sentences are
        not "grammatically" correct; if so done it
        would change the <u>natural</u> rhythm of the story.

About the Author

The Author, a Mother and Grandmother, whose inquiring mind led her through many doors of adventurous learning; Science, Philosophy, Dream Analysis, New Testament Bible Study plus visits to learn and experience new types of therapy classes, ending with Zen Meditation. This led to an "out of the body experience."

She also taught First Grade at a private school for ten years.

Now retired, she shares with you in her first book, **"All In A Nutshell"**, a few of the new and exciting answers to the many questions we ask of ourselves as life unfolds.

Why is life this way? How does it work? What is the purpose and meaning of it all?

In her searching, to her surprise, many of the answers came through the book, "A New Concept of The Universe."

You will be surprised, also, as you travel with her through the explorations of this new usable Wisdom.

www.ingramcontent.com/pod-product-compliance
Lightning Source LLC
Chambersburg PA
CBHW020515290526
45786CB00002B/604